CONFESSION
AND
BOOKKEEPING

CONFESSION AND BOOKKEEPING

The Religious, Moral, and Rhetorical Roots of Modern Accounting

James Aho

State University of New York Press

Published by
State University of New York Press, Albany

For information, address State University of New York Press,
194 Washington Avenue, Suite 305, Albany, NY 12210–2384

Production by Diane Ganeles
Marketing by Susan M. Petrie

Library of Congress Cataloging-in-Publication Data

Aho, James Alfred, 1942–
    Confession and bookkeeping : the religious, moral, and rhetorical roots of modern
accounting / James Aho.
      p. cm.
    Includes bibliographical references and index.
    ISBN 0-7914-6545-4 (hardcover : alk. paper)
    1. Bookkeeping—History. 2. Accounting—Moral and ethical aspects. 3. Capitalism—
Moral and ethical aspects. 4. Economics—Religious aspects—Catholic Church—History. 5.
Christian sociology—Catholic Church—History. I. Title.

HF5635.A265 2005
657'.2'09—dc22

                                                                                    2004027565

10 9 8 7 6 5 4 3 2 1

To my father-in-law,
John W. McMahan

Contents

Preface

In American business schools, accounting is treated primarily as "accountingization" (Power and Laughlin, 1992), that is, as a body of technically refined calculations used by organizations to efficiently accomplish goals such as profit maximization. What, if any, theory that is taught reduces largely to cybernetics and systems theory, approaches eerily detached from the lived-realities of those organizations, even as their recommendations profoundly influence the solidarity, morale, productivity, creativity, and health of those who work in them. As for standard histories of the profession, these are progressivist and functionalist. They reiterate with minor variations a narrative first announced by A. C. Littleton, namely, that since its inception in the fourteenth-century accounting has evolved from "bookkeeping fictions" into "scientific facts" (Littleton, 1933).

For its part the sociology of organizations, which has always had a fond place in its heart for the vibrant underlife of bureaucracies, has become increasingly blind to accounting procedures, which it happily relegates to technical experts. This is a bizarre development indeed, considering that the putative godfather of organizational sociology, Max Weber, essentially defined bureaucracy in terms of modern bookkeeping (Colignon and Covaleski, 1991: 142–43).[1] Richard Colignon and Mark Covaleski attribute organizational sociology's ignorance of accounting to its even more glaring inability to see the zero-sum power relationships that characterize modern corporations. In functionalist organizational theory, domination translates into the innocuous, smiley-faced concept of "leadership," and accounting is treated as simply another technology that promotes benign societal ends (153–54).

A sea-change is now upsetting these academic traditions. Since the early 1990s in the rare and secret precincts where the humanities meet management, European and American accounting theorists have begun writing from a critical historical perspective. Inspired in part by Michel Foucault's idea of "governmentalism"—a convoluted neologism referring to the social control of minds and bodies—they are challenging the socially decontextualized "technocratic pretensions," as one has called them, of their profession (Power and Laughlin, 1992). Following their own independent introduction to Foucault, sociologists have begun reciprocating the gesture, warily reaching out their hands in greeting to their long-lost cousins (cf. Carruthers and Espeland, 1991). Voilà! A critical sociology of accounting is born.

From the standpoint of this emerging interdisciplinary dialogue, accounting is no longer considered only a revelation of the financial realities of an organization. Instead, it is seen as constitutive of that organization's very being. That is to say, accounting is coming to be understood as "making" the very things it pretends to describe, including—through its estimates of equities and assets—a firm's boundaries (Morgan and Willmott, 1993; Hines, 1988). Accounting does this by posing aspects of organizations in monetary terms, disclosing them as "good hard facts." As this occurs, "softer" qualitative factors become irrelevant; in the end, invisible. Accounting procedures establish organization "targets" like the "bottom line" and provide monitoring systems to assess department and personal "outcomes." "Deadwood" is exposed, "rising stars" identified; recommendations are made as to "merit increases" and the infliction of "force reductions." In these ways accounting discourages certain behaviors and investments in certain organizational sectors, while it simultaneously encourages and promotes others.

By compelling workers to attend to organizational "deadlines" and performance "quotas," accounting alters workers' experiences of the procession of events. The speed of lived-time accelerates (Gleick, 1999). Postures rigidify, gait becomes more urgent; skeletal structures and organ function adapt accordingly; health and longevity are affected (Bertman, 1999). What this implies is that far from being a morally and politically neutral enterprise, accounting by its very nature is political: not merely a power tool deployed by elites to aggrandize themselves, which is true enough; but a technology of domination in-itself; a technology legitimized by the ideology of efficiency.

Under the banner of efficiency (cost-effectiveness, profit, etc.) accounting calculations have come to colonize themselves in virtually every institutional realm of modern society from sports, education, and criminal justice, to health-care, war-making, and even religion. The vocabulary of efficiency has been elevated into the "distinctive morality" of our times (Miller and Napier, 1993: 645). Domination has assumed a presumably humane, scientific face; the old forms of coercion have disappeared. Today, each actor wants to do, and freely chooses to do, precisely what efficiency experts recommend. And what they earn from the organization that employs them is mathematically proven to be exactly what they deserve.

ഇൻ

A critical sociology of accounting bases itself on four convictions. The first is that "any way of seeing is also a way of not seeing" (Morgan and Willmott, 1993: 13). In other words, every account of an organizational world, like every set of tinted lenses, highlights some aspects of that world while it veils others, rendering them invisible. Second, it assumes that even the most rational ways of seeing, thinking, and recalling events—of which quantitative accounts are the preeminent example—may in other respects be diabolically unreasonable. That is, they may promote dysfunctional actions, actions that confute the ostensible goals of the organization they report on. This, by distorting information flows, legitimizing incompetency, and inadvertently fostering resistances (Hopwood, 1983: 292–93). A third conviction of a critical sociology of accounting, is that its task is not to be the reification of selected accounting narratives, to make them appear universal, natural, reasonable (and thus irresistible). It is instead to destabilize them, to problematize them, to disturb them (Miller and O'Leary, 1987), or if one prefers, to *destrukt* them (to use Martin Heidegger's more pithy word), so that they can be actively chosen instead of passively suffered. Fourth, it does this by exhibiting that accounting schemes are socially contrived, culturally relative, and historically contingent. To say it in another way, it conducts what Foucault (after Nietzsche) calls "genealogy": showing that what is experienced as a natural fact—such as the quest for precision and efficiency—is in truth an art fact, an artifact, a social construct.

ა∽ა

This book on the moral and religious foundations of double-entry bookkeeping (DEB) is offered as a humble contribution to this four-pronged effort. It begins with the retrieval of a simple, ancient truth: "economics is sacred to the core" (Becker, 1975: 26). Consider the primitive custom known as the potlatch. In this, as in all competitions, participants strive to defeat one another; not, however, by "getting the most" at each other's expense, but by giving it away (Mauss, 1954). Naturally, there is a good bit of debate concerning the meaning of this rite. But the consensus is that in surrendering what is most precious and durable, the celebrants symbolically pay back a debt, or they create obligations on the part of gift recipients. In either case there is an unsaid, yet frank, appreciation of the importance to the human psyche of keeping relations to nature, to the gods, and to the community balanced. To whom much has been given much shall be required, and he who gives much shall receive a comparable amount in kind. Or, as expressed in technical accounting jargon: For every credit there shall be an equal and corresponding debit, and for every debit an equal and corresponding credit. The sum of debits in properly kept books always equates exactly with the summed credits.

While this, the distinguishing equation of DEB, acknowledges an existential truth, evidently it was not formulated in writing until early in the fourteenth century in Italy. This being the case, the circumstances surrounding its written expression constitute a fascinating problem in the sociology of knowledge and, as it turns out, in the sociology of modern consciousness. For just as twentieth-century accounting practices have abetted the social creation of a particular form of governable person, namely, the "efficient worker" (this, through IQ testing, mental hygiene assessments, time-motion studies, and the manipulative practice of negotiated budgeting [Miller and O'Leary, 1987]), DEB was itself complicit in the invention of a new "field of visibility": the Christian merchant. While this is a taken-for-granted reality today, the very thought that a person might be profit-hungry and yet Christian was an outrage to the moral sensibilities of the Middle Ages. Furthermore, because the "invention" of DEB was apparently pivotal in, if not solely responsible for, the emergence of capitalism—an issue I take up later—what might otherwise be considered a small chapter in a minor, esoteric field becomes an archaeology of modern civilization itself. Werner Sombart, whom we will soon meet more formally, goes so far as to equate DEB with the modern sciences of Galileo, Harvey, and Newton. "By the same means, it [DEB] organizes perceptions into a system. . . . Without too much difficulty, we can recognize in double-entry bookkeeping the ideas of gravitation, of the circulation of the blood, and of the conservation matter" (Most, 1976: 23–24). But here, a clarification is in order.

I am not suggesting that DEB *is* modern accounting, a claim still frequently implied by conventional accounting historians (Yamey and Parker, 1994). On the contrary, as accountingization has dispersed itself through society, becoming a sort of contemporary lingua franca, accounting technologies have fragmented. Today, DEB is merely one of an imposing arsenal of operations devised to aid people and organizations to pursue their goals rationally and objectively (Miller and Napier, 1993). Nevertheless, even if DEB is not the basis for all of these procedures, it was certainly the first to promise some degree of mathematical control over organizational resources.

∽∾

The thesis informing this study is that analogous to the ancient potlatch (and the recent advent of social and environmental accounting), DEB arose from a sense of indebtedness on the part of late medieval merchants toward creator, church, and commune. Burdened with this debt, they felt compelled to certify in writing that for everything they earned something of equal value had been returned, and that for everything meted out something else was deserved. Many terms can be used to enframe this sense of indebtedness: "finitude," "limitedness," "creatureliness," "animality," "death consciousness," "lack," "existential evil," and "sin." Since this last is the word that the medieval mind itself typically employed to depict its state, I use it here. To rephrase the preceding proposition, then: DEB arose from a scrupulous preoccupation with sin on the part of the faithful medieval entrepreneur. This, not the least because of his dirty work: profiting from money-lending under questionable circumstances in direct contravention of Church law. This is to say, the medieval merchant found himself in a morally problematic situation that necessitated that he justify himself not only to ecclesiastical authorities, but to these authorities internalized, the voice of his own conscience. To this end he turned easily and naturally to the standard rhetorical models of the day, producing what we now know as DEB. My argument is not that DEB can be used to legitimize commercial activity: a proposition that is now well-established (Carruthers and Espeland, 1991; Gallhofer and Haslam, 1991; McClosky, 1986). It is that DEB was devised by modern Europe's first bookkeepers *expressly* to serve rhetorical ends.[2]

As to the question, what instilled in the merchant's soul such an overweening awareness of personal sin, my answer is: the Roman Catholic sacrament of private penance, or as it is popularly known, confession. Far from being coincidental, the introduction of compulsory confession in 1215 and the appearance of DEB soon thereafter are meaningfully, if not strictly causally, related. The advent of communal chronicling, manorial accounting, the family scrapbook, the personal diary, and so forth, were all elements in a vast accounting enterprise that arose near the end of the Middle Ages. Each in their own way is an exhibit in a larger European project of moral improvement, a project both stimulated by confession and reflected in it.

I am hardly the first to observe a theological component in business record-keeping.[3] It is widely acknowledged that history's first business documents, preserved on clay tablets from Mesopotamian city states (ca. 3000 BCE), concerned almost exclusively temple purchases and disbursements (Oppenheim,

1964: 231). In all of the major world religions, furthermore—Zoorastrianism (*Pahlavi Texts*, part I, 30.4–33), Judaism (Deut., 7.9–11), Islam (Qur'an, s. 17, v. 13), and Buddhism (*Tibetan Book of the Dead*, 75)—divine judges keep ledgers on their communicants. Following their deaths, the moral balances of each are said to be weighed in the scales of justice to determine their fates in the hereafter. The Book of Revelations in fact alludes to a kind of *double*-entry bookkeeping. Each person's credits and debits, we are told, are entered not just once, but twice: first in the Book of Accounts, a judicial record kept on earth by humanity, and again in the Book of Life, a register of citizenship in the heavenly Jerusalem (Rev., 20.11–15). All of this is to say nothing of medieval penitential literature that abounds with references to a divine "Auditor" who hears accounts. One can also find remarkably modern assertions like the following, attributed to Pope Cyprian (252 CE): "The blood of martyrs he [the penitent] can carry to his "credit" [*in acceptum referre alicui*], as the businessman can his gifts, interest earnings, and gambling winnings" (Watkins, 1920: I, 209).

Nor did the conflation of business and moral/spiritual accounting disappear after the Reformation. Far from it. Methodist Church founder John Wesley, Daniel DeFoe, Samuel Pepys, Baptist evangelicals, the deist Benjamin Franklin, the Shakers, Harmony Society, and more recently, the Iona Community in Britain, all (have) insist(ed) that the keeping of meticulous financial accounts is part and parcel of a more general program of honesty, orderliness, and industriousness, which is to say, of Protestant rectitude (Jacobs and Walker, 2000; Maltby, 1997; Walker, 1998; Weber, 1958: 124). Late eighteenth-century bookkeeping instructors advised that

> if the necessary regularity in keeping accounts is observed; . . . a man call tell at one view whether his manner of living is suited to his fortune, [and] he will consequently be enabled to form a proper medium for adjusting his expenses to his income, by which means he may be guarded against . . . the evils of intemperance; from whence flow so many vices. . . . (Yamey, 1949: 104–5)

Today, of course, at least in business, references to morality and religion in accounting are rare. Nonetheless, as the
recent Enron-Fannie Mae-Tyko-MCI-Global Crossing-Lucent-
Tenet Healthcare-WorldCom-RiteAid-Health South-Arthur
Anderson-Bristol Myers Squibb-Halliburton scandals demonstrate, corporations continue to "cook" books to inflate profits (or to hide them from tax collectors). Indeed, today it is
hard to remember that accounting is more than an exercise in
smoke and mirrors, the dubious profession of artful dodging
(Mitchell, Sikka, and Willmott, 1998). In other words, while
accounting may have forgotten its religious and moral roots, it
continues to have persuasive, rhetorical functions.

੭ഗ

Finally, a few comments on the epistemological status of this
study. Sociology has come a long way from presuming to
describe and explain the world from a position of omniscient
neutrality. Today, it is expected that practitioners of the discipline reflexively apply the notions and ideas they impose on
others to themselves. For my purposes this means acknowledg-
ing that sociology is at heart a style—or more accurately,
styles—of storytelling (for unlike physics or biology there is no
grand narrative that all sociologists agree is worth relating). In
other words, sociology is an exercise in accounting, and like all
accounts it renders social reality in/visible, highlighting certain
facets of our lives together while blinding us to others. In the
following pages I elucidate the moral/rhetorical/religious components of DEB, while remaining silent about its well-
researched financial utility in banking, or its connection to
printing technologies. Thus, while I hope mine is an engaging
story, one that inspires recognition, a reknowing of what was
already dimly perceived and thought, it makes no claims to be
the final word about an accounting format that has been so
important for all of us.

　　As just pointed out, accounts never just describe the
world. "In communicating reality, we construct reality"
(Hines, 1988). What, it may be asked, is the reality I wish to
accomplish here? It is, simply, to encourage a more pious,
thankful attitude toward the larger community, toward history,

and toward the universe on the part of those who have enjoyed its benefice. It is to help undermine a doctrine that has been elevated into a virtual cant in our era, namely, that the highest human virtue is selfishness (Rand, 1961) or, as posed in subtler terms, "the only social responsibility of business is to increase its profits" (Friedman, 1970). In other words, I want to promote in place of these popular dogmas a sense of grateful stewardship and responsibility to a cosmos that makes profit—and indeed, egotism itself—possible in the first place, by showing that at one time gratitude was exactly the prevailing sentiment.

Acknowledgments

The one person most responsible for this book being in print is Kerry Jacobs, professor of accounting in the School of Business at La Trobe University, Melbourne, Australia. I had long given up on the project when out of the blue Professor Jacobs (then at Edinburgh University in Scotland) e-mailed me in spring 2003 requesting a copy of an article on medieval bookkeeping—here, the basis of chapter 7—that had been published eighteen years earlier. Jacobs wrote something to the effect that he could hardly believe that any sociologist, much less an American—American sociology has a less than vaunted reputation in Europe—could or would study bookkeeping. I, in turn, was astounded to learn that a business professor was conducting ethnographic field research on, of all things, religious orders. This shock was doubled when Jacobs informed me that in Great Britain, the discipline of business administration had appropriated Marxism, social linguistics, critical theory, and Foucauldian sociology into its outlook. Thus began an intense exchange of communications: Jacobs sending me extensive lists of to-reads; I reciprocating with observations on his work. This book has grown from interdisciplinary collaboration of the best sort.

As for the original project, it emerged from conversations—not all of which I understood at the time—with my late father-in-law, John W. McMahan, then an accountant for the Atomic Energy Commission. To my knowledge at least, he was the first recipient of the Ph.D. in accounting in America (McMahan, 1939). His dissertation traces parallels between the logic of modern bookkeeping and Thomistic philosophy. It is the inspiration for, if not the thesis of, this book. In my personal library sits Dr. McMahan's dog-eared, pencil-marked copy of what is still one of the most readable and comprehensive social histories of accounting every written, that authored by his major adviser, A. C. Littleton.

I could have accomplished little academically were it not for the generosity and indulgence of my often befuddled colleagues at Idaho State University (ISU) ("What is he up to now?"). Much of the initial research for this project, conducted at the University of New Mexico, was undertaken with the help of an ISU faculty research grant. My wife, poet Margaret Aho, translated selections in Latin from several medieval home economics textbooks.

I am grateful for permission to use parts of a previously published article as a chapter in this book: "Rhetoric and the Invention of Double Entry Bookkeeping." Reproduced by permission from the University of California Press from *Rhetorica: A Journal of the History of Rhetoric* 3 (winter 1985): 21–43. © International Society for the History of Rhetoric.

CHAPTER 1

The Problem

The conditions giving rise to rational bureaucratic capitalism, or to what Max Weber calls "the most fateful force in modern life" (Weber, 1958: 17), remain perennially interesting to social historians. What follows is a sociology of one of its pivotal features, double-entry bookkeeping (DEB). My object is to show how this calculative practice emerged from the moral milieu of the late Middle Ages; how Roman Catholic moral theology insinuated itself into commerce via sacramental confession; and how both commerce and morality were changed as a result: morality becoming, as it were, commercialized (more accommodating to the merchant), and commerce "Christianized."

I am not arguing that confession *caused* DEB in a mechanistic way. Nor am I searching for the "origin" of DEB in medieval business records, à la conventional accounting historiography. Instead, I am concerned with weaving DEB into a larger social/cultural context, showing how what appears to be simply another mathematical technology once had great religious and moral significance.

In taking up this subject, I grapple with an argument first advanced by Weber, and that eighty years later has become virtually a dogmatic injunction in sociology, namely, that Catholicism has been (and remains) a poor host to the forces of economic change. By implication, I confirm the thesis promulgated by Weber's not always friendly adversary, Werner Sombart. Relying on his understanding—which Weber rebuked as giving "a painful impression of superficiality"—of Thomistic moral theology, Sombart shows that far from being inimical to the rational pursuit of wealth, medieval Catholicism actually encouraged it (Sombart, 1924; cf. Nussbaum, 1937). While historians (some of whom are cited later) have since tempered Weber's argument, providing independent corroboration of Sombart's claim (cf. McGovern, 1970), with few exceptions their findings have yet to penetrate the reaches of popular sociology.[1]

This book addresses a subject that to my knowledge, at least, few if any sociologists have ever addressed: accounting procedures. As mentioned in the preface, structural functionalism and its stepchild, organizational sociology, traditionally have displayed a blithe indifference to calculative technologies in business, taking it for granted that "the formal rationality of accounting, . . . is built into the nature of things, [as] the perfection of the means for achieving societal ends; ends which [to them] are self-evident[ly]" valid and good (Colignon and Covaleski, 1991: 153). Richard Colignon and Mark Covaleski suggest that this complacency grows from the politically compromised status of functionalists and organizational sociologists as research handmaidens to corporate management. However this may be, the following pages are intended as a corrective to this bias. It problematizes what heretofore has been passed over with silence by my own discipline.

Weber and Sombart on Penance

The narratives of Weber and Sombart occupy a middle range between abstract theory and particularism. Instead of attempting to derive economic activity from the ideal-typical (read: nonexistent) utility maximizer, or of remaining at a purely descriptive level, both seek to trace the psyche of the medieval merchant back to a specific institutional setting, the workings of which are susceptible to indirect observation. And for both of them, the locus out of which the late medieval mind is presumed to have arisen is the sacrament of penance. The Weber-Sombart controversy, as inherited by us, revolves around their conflicting interpretations of the meaning of this ritual for its participants.

To Weber, it was the "sacrament of absolution," as he calls it, which explains why "inner-worldly asceticism," the heart of the "capitalist spirit" (a term I discuss later) allegedly failed to flourish in the Catholic world. Sombart disagrees. It was precisely this sacrament, he submits, which nurtured an incipient capitalist spirit in Catholic lands; a spirit which, when implanted in the fertile soil of the Italian trading centers, burst into history's first modern business enterprises.

In his sociology of religion, Weber distinguishes between the systematic effort by the individual to secure his or her own salvation on the one hand, and the distribution grace through "magical sacraments" on the other, wherein devotees are relegated to passively observing the manipulations of priests. In Protestantism, where the first salvific technique prevails, radical ethical conversion—today's so-called born again experience—is common. In Catholicism, by contrast, where the second form predominates, "the level of personal ethical accomplishment must . . . be made compatible with average human qualifications," which is to say, "quite low" (Weber, 1963: 151–53). According to Weber, the Catholic "priest was a magician of sorts who performed the miracle of transubstantiation and who held the key to eternal life in his hand. . . . He dispensed atonement, hope of grace, certainty of forgiveness, and thereby granted release from the tremendous tension to which the Calvinist was doomed by an inexorable fate, admitting of no mitigation . . ." (1958: 117).

Although, he continues, the distribution of grace in Catholicism could in principle have encouraged ascetic rigor (were its reception made contingent upon the recipient publicly demonstrating their virtue), the sacrament of penance rendered this unnecessary. This is because instead of magnifying the believer's sense of personal responsibility for wrongdoing, it mollified it, sparing him or her the necessity of developing a planned pattern of life based on the Decalogue.

With his acute sensitivity to detail, Weber admits that this characterization "in a certain sense" does "violence to historical reality." He nonetheless insists that apart from the monastic orders (Weber, 1958: 118–19), the heterodox teachings of Duns Scotus (235, n. 76), and the pre-Reformation sects of Wyclif and Hus (198, n. 12), the "normal medieval Catholic layman lived ethically, so to speak from hand to mouth," in "the very human cycle of sin, repentance, atonement, release, followed by renewed sin" (117). In any case, whatever asceticism St. Ignatius, the monks of Cluny, the Cistercians, or the Franciscans practiced, it was not undertaken to reform the world, à la Calvinism, but to flee from it altogether.[2]

Sombart disputes this. "The capitalist spirit," he says, "first manifested itself in Renaissance Italy," approximately two centuries *before* Martin Luther nailed his theses to the door of Castle Church in 1517. And this spirit reached its apogee in the Tuscan republics, of which the city-state of Florence was the most important. In answer to the question, why? he replies that Florentine merchants not only were influenced by classical philosophers like Cicero, Seneca, and Livy; more importantly, they were devoted Catholics. "The origins of capitalism made their appearance at a time when the Church held sway over men's minds . . ." (Sombart, 1967: 228–29). And "it is of supreme interest to note that religious zeal was nowhere so hot and strong as in Florence" (229).

> Finally, we must not forget how mighty a weapon the Catholic Church possessed in the confessional. . . . We must suppose that the businessman discussed with his father-confessor the principles that governed his economic activities. Do we not know that numerous treatises were written, advising the clergy how to guide their flocks in all that affects life, even to the minutest detail? (230–31)

The issue is thus squarely posed. Either the sacrament of penance inhibited a lifestyle conducive to rational bureaucratic acquisition or it did not. This book intends to help resolve this dispute once and for all. Which is not to say that as they stand, either Weber's or Sombart's views are immune from criticism. On the contrary, knowledge of the actual dynamics and behavioral consequences of penance seems to have remained for both largely a mystery hidden behind the black curtains of the confessional booth. Indeed, to the ordinary Catholic their depictions of confession appear stereotypical to the point of banality. Take Weber.

Weber claims that all of the essentials of Catholic sacramental life, including confession, "have been fixed since the time of Gregory the Great" (reigned 590–604 CE) (Weber, 1963: 188). We now know that this is incorrect. True, in his acute awareness of the pastoral needs of penitents Gregory appears to have anticipated something on the lines of confession. But he was addressing a ritual technically known as Mediterranean or canonical penance, which is fundamentally different from the sacrament of confession that is my interest in these pages. As we shall see momentarily, the roots of confession are to be found in Celtic monastic life, not in Roman courtrooms; it was not recognized in Church law until six centuries after Gregory's death.

That Weber is not completely unaware of the evolution from canonical penance to confession is suggested by his reference to the penitential handbooks that were routinely cited by priests hearing confessions to estimate punishments for sins. However, he dismisses their importance by viewing them merely as efforts to "combine the techniques of Roman law with the Teutonic conception of fiscal expiation (wergild)" (Weber, 1963: 190). This view has since been thoroughly rejected as a result of detailed examination of passages from these handbooks. Chapter 2 discusses some of the relevant findings.

Sombart is also guilty of oversights regarding penance that have led him astray. To begin with, the "numerous treatises" to which he refers in the previous quotation, evidently are not the penitential handbooks, which unlike Weber he seems unacquainted with, but various *summa theologica* and *morale* of three Church doctors: Thomas Aquinas (c. 1274), Antonino of Florence (d. 1459), and Bernardino of Siena (d. 1444) (Sombart, 1967: 383, n. 278). To justify his choice of these names, Sombart points out that besides their all being Italian (although Aquinas spent his career in Paris), these were not "mild bookworms unlearned in the ways of the world, abstruse thinkers of the cloisters and the study, engaged in hair-splitting and endless repetitions concerning unrealities" (243–44). This is true, but irrelevant. The fact is that Bernardino and Antonino both not only wrote long after Italian capitalism was already flourishing; they were canonized and popularized much later than this. It would hardly be logical, then, to attribute causal influence to their teachings on the behavior of those who lived a century before their time. The case of St. Thomas, of course, is different. He was canonized in 1323, and his theology became sacrosanct in Dominican orders around the very time that DEB was first being introduced (i.e., ca. 1340). However, as recent studies have shown, it is a grave mistake to rely on formal theological treatises to draw pictures of lay behavior. Even conceding that St. Thomas indirectly might have influenced economic affairs during his life, as to the direct use of his writings (or those of any other scholastic) in confession: this was even less likely in the thirteenth and fourteenth centuries than it is today. This, for no other reason than they were disseminated in Latin for university audiences, not in the vernacular for common folk. The available evidence indicates that it was the penitential handbooks mentioned by Weber, not theological texts, which were employed by pastors in confession; these typically are devoid of any moral theorizing whatsoever. Instead, they consist of highly stylized, easily memorizable injunctions and interrogatory devices.

While Weber and Sombart both attempt to situate the medieval economic ethos in a specific institutional matrix, the inference leaps that they make from moral teachings to business practices are best heroically gymnastic; at worst they are unconvincing. It takes a particularly astute reader of *The Protestant Ethic*, for example, to bridge the gap between Weber's discussion of John Calvin (who profoundly mistrusted material acquisition), his treatment of the Reverend Richard Baxter's seventeenth-century homilies (which endorse the connection between wealth and virtue), and the content of the worldly deist Benjamin Franklin's *Advice to a Young Tradesman*. The links that Sombart draws between Thomistic theology and capitalist values are even less persuasive. Sombart argues that Thomism penetrated Italian commerce through advice proffered in various scrapbooks kept by prominent Florentine and Venetian families (Sombart, 1967: 375–76, n. 141). The most famous of these was Leon Battista Alberti's *Del Governo della Famiglia* (1443), "a classic in its own time." In its celebration of thrift as holy, says Sombart, it anticipates Benjamin Franklin and Daniel DeFoe both in substance and in form (101–14). Weber (I think, correctly) repudiates Sombart for "seriously misinterpreting" the meaning of the scrapbooks for their audiences. He points out that for all Alberti's advocacy of industriousness, scheduling, and the keeping of accounts, in reality he shunned acquisition beyond what would be necessary to maintain one's social position. The pursuit of wealth for Alberti, in other words, was not a religious calling as it allegedly was for the Calvinist.[3] More to the point, Alberti cites the pagan philosophers Cicero, Horace, and Xenophon to justify his fatherly preachments, more than he does any Church dogmatist. St. Thomas, for example, is never mentioned. How Alberti's Christian faith actually bore on his practical advice if it did at all, then, remains an open question.

What this all adds up to is a need to reexamine the lived-world of the medieval denizen: not from the outside, but analogous to Weber's own incomparable phenomenology of the Calvinist psyche; from the inside, from the viewpoint of the medieval merchant himself. To accomplish this will require more than merely depicting how the moral teachings of confession bore upon the merchant (as important as this is), as Sombart does (however poorly). It will also be necessary to ponder on how the ritual of the sacrament itself was conducted and how its procedures might have impacted the medieval soul. These are my intentions.

Weber and Sombart on Accounting

Weber and Sombart both claim that the introduction of DEB was essential for the emergence of modern capitalism. Indeed, Weber goes so far as to define modern capitalism in terms of DEB. A modern firm is "one with capital accounting, that is, an establishment which determines its income yielding power by calculation according to the methods of modern bookkeeping and the striking of balance" (Weber, 1950: 275; 1947, 50–51; 1958, 21–22). Sombart concurs with this, saying that "one can not imagine what capitalism would be without double-entry bookkeeping: the two phenomena are connected as intimately as form and contents" (Sombart, 1924: 118). DEB operationalizes the idea of economic gain in terms of a specific quantity, namely, money; and it allows a firm to trace its financial progress over time, enabling its owners to adjust their behavior in response to changing market circumstances. It also allows them to calculate the overall assets of the business, its obligations to creditors, and to determine dividend shares to partners on a basis proportional to their contributions.

The foremost historian of the subject, Basil Yamey (1949, 1964), among others (e.g., Winjum, 1970; Most, 1972; Carruthers and Espeland, 1991) considers the Weber/Sombart assertions to be "greatly exaggerated." As we shall see in chapter 3, the recommendations of period textbooks indicate that while DEB could be deployed in such a way as to promote rational decision-making, more likely it was used primarily to insure that business records were complete and accurately kept, period. Nonetheless, even Yamey and others agree that DEB always harbored the potential to do the things attributed to it by Weber and Sombart. And just what are these things?

Acquisitiveness, Weber argues, is universal. Even rationally mediated earning or capitalism proper, where each act is predicated upon the probability of maximizing profit, was well-known in precolonial India, the ancient Mediterranean, the Muslim world, and China. What distinguishes modern profit-making from more primitive species of the phenomenon are two things: the separation of business from the home and capital accounting: the ". . . valuation of the total assets of the enterprise, . . . at the beginning of an [accounting period]; and the comparison of this with a similar valuation . . . at the end of the process" (Weber, 1947: 191–92).

Weber goes on to attribute the introduction of capital accounting to a "capitalist spirit." This, instead of explaining it as a product exclusively of material and technical circumstances—for instance, algebra, the number naught, joint partnerships, and money exchanges. By capitalist spirit he means a culturally specific way of being in the world; an emotional and cognitive habit of formal rationality, *Zweckrationalitat*, wherein different means to an end are weighed in terms of their respective costs (the closest English equivalent is "utilitarianism"). He contrasts this mind-set with substantive, ends-orientated rationality *(Wertrationalitat)* in which, regardless of its costs, any action is considered appropriate if it serves a particular end (Weber, 1947: 115, n. 38).

Sombart agrees with Weber that the crucial generative factor of modern accounting was ideational. Furthermore, while he poses his discussion in somewhat looser terms than Weber, he insists that what is distinctive to the capitalist spirit is not its "silken woof," the desire for monetary gain, but its "cotton warp," the predisposition to earn money in a "bourgeois" way (Sombart, 1967: 22), that is, by means of calculative exactness *(Rechenhaftigkeit)*. This is "the tendency, the habit, perhaps more—the capacity to think of the universe in terms of figures, and to transform these figures into a well-knit system of income and expenditure" (125). While the Protestant burgher of England, Germany, and the Netherlands definitely exemplified this characterology, says Sombart (once more agreeing with Weber), so did the late medieval (Catholic) Italian merchant. As to the question, why? Sombart invokes what Weber dismisses as "a thesis in the worst sense." The Italian merchant class, says Sombart, was bourgeoisified through its participation in the primary agency of Catholic moral discipline, the sacrament of penance.

It is not necessary to restate the objections to Sombart's argument. As one of his biographers notes, although *Der Moderne Kapitalismus* is "an exciting and challenging book, valid facts and unreliable information stand side by side in *liaisons dangereuses*" (Kuczynaski, 1968). It is enough to say that my purpose in this book is to expand on and enrich Sombart's proposition without stumbling into the same pitfalls.

As for the errors in Weber's history of DEB, these are not just dangerous (as they are with Sombart); they are deadly.

This, because they reinforce the basis of his entire argument that within the Christian cosmos only Protestantism could have sired modern capitalism.

To support his contention, Weber cites the "Dutch theorist Simon Stevin" as the person who "first insisted upon . . . the device of the balance" in 1698 (Weber, 1950: 207). Ignoring the fact that Stevin died in 1620, it is now commonly acknowledged that DEB and the drawing of balance were in use two centuries prior to the Reformation, and then in the Catholic cities of Florence, Genoa, and Venice (Cohen, 1980: 1345–47). In fact the first textbook on the subject, which Stevin himself draws upon, was authored by none other than a Franciscan monk; a book written several decades before Stevin was born. In other words, far from being a product of the Calvinist spirit, DEB emerged from the culture of the high Middle Ages, when through her sacramental regulation of the total life course of the individual, Roman Catholicism dominated the European psyche as never before.

How Weber could have committed such a grave error in regard to the dating of DEB is a matter for others to determine. For one thing, the Massari ledgers of Genoa (dated ca. 1340), which provide the first bona fide example of DEB, were not made available (and then in Italian) until 1909, five years after first installment of *The Protestant Ethic* was published. Yet, Weber's own doctoral dissertation plainly reveals that he had carefully gone over the books of two prominent Florentine family businesses, those of the Alberti and the Peruzzi (Weber, 2003: 160–66). There, he notes that while the ledgers are presented "in a dilettante way," they show how interest on loans to partners were accounted for and how, every two years, shares of the companies' profits were meted out in proportion to the partners' equity shares of capital. In other words, by his own admission, the accounts demonstrate that the families' bookkeepers were able to "calculate according to the methods of modern bookkeeping" which, as we just saw, Weber considers the sine qua non of modern capitalism. (Weber fails to mention whether or not the ledger items were posted dually. Those in the Alberti books probably were; those of the Peruzzi's, however, were not [Roover, 1958: 33–34].) The point, however, is not to decry Weber's oversight or contradiction, whatever its source; it is to correct it. This is my goal in the pages to follow.

CHAPTER 2

Roman Catholic Penance

History

Virtually from the moment of its founding, Christianity has
endorsed the practice of penance both for the debasement of
self and its purification. Not until 1215, however, under the
auspices of Pope Innocent III and the Fourth Lateran Council,
did a particular kind of penance, this involving the confession
of one's sins to a priest, become law. Up to this time the recognized, if rarely used, penitential rite was known as canonical penance. This did not involve the divulgence of sins so
much as the conferral of a status, excommunication, which
was grudgingly granted by bishops upon request by candidates
themselves. Canonical penance was permitted only once after
baptism, and for reasons listed in the following section it was
usually undertaken only by the exceptionally religious (or
exhibitionistic).

To be sure, the Church was already employing a kind of
private consultation with priests for *therapeutic* (as opposed
to strictly salvific purposes) as early as the third century
(Tentler, 1977: 20–21). But not until the fifth and sixth centuries is there evidence of a confessional ceremony for the
absolution of sins proper. And this is found not in the Christian heartland of continental Europe, but in Celtic monasteries
lying on the western reaches of the civilized world (Watkins,
1920: II, 578–632; McNeill, 1932b).[1] It was the Celtic rite
that the Fourth Lateran Council would recognize as compulsory for all believers, on pain of being "barred from entrance
to the church" while alive, and "when dying . . . [of being]
deprived a church burial" (Denzinger, 1957: 173, sec. 437;
Watkins, 1920: II, 733–34, 748–49).

13

The handbooks used in the original Celtic confessional betray the influence of the so-called pillar saints and desert fathers of the ancient Syrian Church. The regimens of the latter in turn presumably are traceable to the influence of Hinduism (McNeill and Gamer, 1938: 3). (The period of Hindu cultural expansion in the Near East [ca. 320–570 CE] took place coterminous with the rise of Christian monasticism; it is worth noting that the Gaelic word *amnchara* [spiritual director] has the same root as the Sanskrit *acharya*.) It was also in Syrian monasteries where medical metaphors, later used by Irish confessors to prescribe *medicamenta* for sins, were first introduced.

Whatever its alleged sources, Celtic penance involved the submission of a novice to an older "soul friend." To this were wedded sometimes brutal injunctions from Canon Law and the Celtic folkway of compensation *(eric)*, including mind-numbing recitations of psalms (which John McNeill and Helena Gamer compare to the penitential singing of the Brahmana codes in Hinduism [McNeill and Gamer, 1938: 27]), sleep deprivation by means of cold-water baths, stinging nettles, being placed in a coffin with a corpse, being scantily clad in frigid weather, flagellation, fasting on bread and water, solitary confinement, and in the most serious cases, exile (30–35).

After its appearance in the Celtic world, private penance spread rapidly to Burgundy, Lombardy, and Switzerland (by 650 CE), to Saxon England (by 670 CE), and to Germany by the end of the first millennium. By the eighth century there is mention of persons of high rank having their own private confessors. Some bishops, sensing a challenge to their monopoly to absolve sins, railed against the procedure as "play-acting inanity, which carnal men presume to sanction" (Poschmann, 1964: 139; cf. 131–34). They defamed the penitential handbooks used in confession as "filled with errors and composed by unworthy authors" (Orsy, 1978: 43). In 829 CE the Council of Paris went so far as to order the books burned, but it was too late. The futility of resisting such a popular custom had become evident already to most Church authorities.

Among the reasons for the enthusiastic reception of confession was that canonical penance (the earlier rite) had fallen into ill-fame and had practically disappeared by the ninth century. This is because while its object had been to promote moral discipline, its very rigors—which included a decade long excommunication, complete abstinence, the donning of hair shirts and ashes, the forswearing of marriage, public office, and the priesthood—tended to encourage the opposite. While an exemplary few might use the rite to theatrically display their piety before the congregation, the average believer tended to avoid it as long as possible, sometimes until the deathbed itself. As early as the fifth century, Pope Innocent I (reigned 401–77 CE) was conceding that under the auspices of the canonical rite it was possible for a person to "have surrendered on every occasion to the pleasures of incontinence, and at the end of their lives ask for [absolution] . . . meanwhile [continuing to enjoy] the reconciliation of communion" (Denzinger, 1957: 41: sec. 95).

McNeill believes that apart from Hindu asceticism, the precursor of Celtic penance was Greek medicine (McNeill, 1932b, 1934). The penitential handbook authored by Finnian (ca. 525 CE) announces it clearly: The object of confession is not to punish the penitent's faults as much as it is to cure his or her soul *(cura animarum)*. He writes of sin as less an outward act, than as an "illness" of which the act is a mere "symptom." As such, the penalties are not conceived as *noxae vindicta* in the Roman sense, but as *remedia* or *fomenta* (poultices). (Later commentaries would go so far as to attribute specific physical diseases to their causes in immorality. Heart disease was said to be due to pride, for example; frenzy to anger, leprosy to envy, and epilepsy to lechery [Bloomfield,1952: 373].)

According to Finnian, the medicines prescribed by spiritual physicians are not intended to punish outward acts after the fact, but to quell inward thoughts. "Thought evil and intended to do it, but opportunity failed him"; "has frequently entertained (evil) thoughts and hesitated to act on them"; "has sinned in the thoughts of his heart"; or "plotted in his heart": all of these are worthy of confession, he argues. For while they remain hidden from the eyes of men, they are known to God (Finnian, 1938: secs. 1–17). By the same token, while an outwardly wrongful act may be regrettable, if it is committed without consciousness of its immorality, is done under duress, or is an accident, the penitent is counseled not to hold themselves blameworthy.

Although intentionality was acknowledged in the Celtic penitentials, the theory behind it was not formulated until much later. Indeed, as late as the twelfth century, Abbot Bernard criticized the monks of Clairvaux for what he considered their narcissistic preoccupation with their own internal states; he admonished them to focus on their remorse instead on what they actually did. The turn toward a moral theology of intentionality had to await the appearance of Abelard (d. 1142), the renown teacher and rather more infamous seducer of the aristocratic maiden, Heloise (Delumeau, 1990: 197).

Abelard's doctrine of intentionality affected European consciousness in profound, largely unanticipated, ways. For it compelled the average believer to begin exploring regions of their own subjectivity that heretofore had been secreted in darkness except for a minority of religious athletes. Irrespective of any specific moral rules it promoted, in other words, it helped disclose a new range of visibility to the ordinary Christian, the intricacies of their own souls. Just as the microscope would soon reveal the cellular shadow-lands of corporeality, and the telescope the outreaches of the universe (in both cases destabilizing the received world), interior confession laid the groundwork for the eventual appearance of what today is known as depth psychology (Foucault, 1978: 68; Nelson, 1981: 49–54).

To be sure, Abelard's rendering of confession was not the only notion to prefigure the likes of Schopenhauer, Nietzsche, Freud, Adler, and Jung. The stoic philosopher, Seneca (4 BCE–65 CE), to name just one, was recommending the daily introspection of conscience (and the divulgence of such investigations to one's superior) as early as the time of Christ, over a thousand years prior to the advent of penitential confession (Foucault, 1988). However, there is little evidence that Seneca's teachings, or those of any other pagan thinker, had any direct bearing either on confession or on modern psychology.

The bishop to whom one applied for penitential excommunication under the the ancient rite of canonical penance was permitted mercy in his sentencing on the basis of his knowledge of the circumstances surrounding the candidate's sins, including their state of mind. This is certain. But he was not encouraged to be so; in any case, he was not so obliged by law. This is a far cry from the immensely more psychologically nuanced practice of Celtic penance. "Just as physicians of bodies prepare their remedies in various sorts," writes St. Columban, "so therefore spiritual physicians ought heal with various sorts of treatments the sorrows, sicknesses and infirmities of the soul" (Columban, 1938: secs. A-12 and B). St. Bede agrees: "All are not to be weighed in one and the same balance but there is discrimination for each [case] . . ." (McNeill, 1932b: 24). The father confessor is admonished to be acutely sensitive to everything associated with the penitent's acts: their number, the perpetrator's state of mind, their where and when, the means of their commitment, and the victim's status. Furthermore, he is urged to take into consideration the degree of contriteness exhibited by the penitent, their intelligence or lack thereof, their past habits, age, gender, social rank, and even health. After all, the father-confessor is not an impersonal administrator of an abstract legal code, but a sympathetic minister to wounded souls. And while an excess of lenience may be insufficient to bring the penitent to a proper state of guilt and shame, a ruthless application of severities may aggravate their condition. In any case, "no physician can treat the wounds of the sick unless he familiarizes himself with their foulness" (23, cf. 25–26).

To be effectively treated, it was believed that moral infirmities had to be rebalanced by their contrary virtues: *Contraria contrariis sanantur* (contraries are cured by contraries). Here is glimpsed the most obvious influence of Greek medicine on confession. For the Greek physicians Methodius and Hypocrites also held that robust health entails an equilibrium of sorts between hot and cold fluids, moist and dry vapors, angry and placid moods, and so on. So "if a cleric is covetous," advises Finnian, "it can be corrected by liberality and alms-giving" (Finnian, 1938: secs. 28 and 29). And if, agrees St. Columban, he suffers from gluttony, then let him be cured by fasting; if lust, then by abstinence; if envy, by restraint of tongue (Columban, 1938: secs. A-12 and B; cf. McNeill and Gamer, 1938: 321–45).

It is likely that the theory of Greek medicine was received by ancient Syrian monks through their work in hospitals. One account claims that it was subsequently broadcast to Celtic brothers via the itinerant monk, John Cassian (ca. 360–434 CE) (Mitchell, 1955: 11–12; McNeill, 1932b: 16–19). Cassian is also credited for introducing to Irish penance the idea of the seven (or eight, depending on one's reading) deadly sins, each of which is said to arise from the preceding and to lead to the next (Bloomfield, 1952: 69–72). Cassian depicts pride *(superbia)* as "the fountainhead of all evil," or to use a more colorful metaphor, the "beast" who "captains the devil's army." From it the others—envy, wrath, sloth, avarice, gluttony, and lust— follow in "military order." Each sin in turn is divided into its "children" or "species," and each of these graded in terms of their seriousness. This system is found virtually unchanged in penitential handbooks down to our time.

Dissemination

In the decades after 1215 few didactic devices were ignored by the Church in her attempt to instill in the lay soul a sense of the new sacrament, each adapted to the inclinations, needs, and abilities of the audience (Delumeau, 1990: 198–211). First came a spate of Dominican *summa pastoralis, confessorum,* and *casibus* (casuistry) (Michaud-Quantin, 1962: 15–43). Then, following the death of Thomas Aquinas in 1274, a new generation of manuals was devised, citing earlier cases and analyzing new ones in light of the opinions of *doctores moderni* (Boyle, 1974: 245–68). With the formal treatises appeared an even greater number of abbreviated vernacular versions for use by pastors in confession (Dondain, 1937; Simmons and Nolloth, 1901; MacKinnon, 1969; Page, 1976). Soon thereafter came numerological devices to aid penitents in composing complete confessions (Francis, 1968 [1942]; Dondain, 1937:

10–11, 217–18) and prepackaged homilies citing legendary authorities, illustrated with moral anecdotes of local interest (Wenzel, 1976). There were moralized picture-stories of the seven major sins and their "whelps," "retainers," and "poisonous serpents" for use as mnemonic devices (Wilson, 1954: 54–64, 83–87; Bloomfield, 1952: 76–84, 103, 249). There were even catchy songs and ditties (Clark, 1905; Thompson, 1940: 257–58; MacKinnon, 1969: 40–45). According to Thomas Tentler, the sheer mass and variety of penitential literature "proves its intellectual significance." It was, he says, the most frequently mentioned and widest read material in Christendom prior to the sixteenth century (Tentler, 1977: 28–51; Bloomfield, 1955).[2]

A Penitential Ditty

The seuen deadly synnes I can not excuse:
    For I am gylty, in many man or wise,
With delectation, consente, and use;
    Al now to reherse I may not suffyse;
In pryde, enuye, wrath, lechery & covetyse,
    Sleuth, and glotony, with all her spices,
Alas! Al my life is full of vices.

From Clark, 1905: part 1, lines 162–68.

It is the vernacular texts that concern me here, for it is they that directly influenced the average churchgoer. Allowing for differences in format, style, and language, all of them insist on the following points.[3] Penance is required of all believers beyond the age of discretion (ca. 12) at least once a year, preferably more often. This, with a priest not necessarily of their own parish. It consists of three parts: contrition, confession proper, and satisfaction. Contrition involves a painstaking "examination and recollection" by the penitent of their past. In it they are to reflect on the "gravity of [their] sins, [their] multitude, [and their] baseness." Contemplating the likelihood of eternal damnation if they fail to do so, the penitent must firmly resolve to amend their ways. To this end, they are cautioned to be "diligently exact" in their self-examination, "search[ing] all the nooks and recesses of [their] conscience," lest one mortal sin escape purview. (Some handbooks recommend that if the confessor appears unprepared in this regard, they should be refused absolution.) After rehearsing their case, penitents must approach the sitting priest and in the sight of all—the private booth would come later—clearly, frankly, and humbly disclose their sins; not, it must be emphasized, their "sins in general only," but "one by one," according to their species and number, situating each in the circumstances that occasioned it. This includes not only acts done in public and those in secret, but "even those of thought." (These generally include the seven deadly sins and their "children," those against the ten commandments, those of the five senses, those against the three theological virtues, the seven sacraments, the four cardinal virtues, the seven gifts of the holy spirit, the eight beatitudes, and the twelve articles of faith.) If any sin in thought or deed is concealed whether out of despair, shame, fear, hope for a long life, or forgetfulness, then it remains unforgiven. (Thus, the encouragement that confession be prompt and frequent). "For if one who is ill is ashamed to make known his wound to the physician," it cannot be treated. To facilitate full divulgence, the priest is advised to discretely, but assertively interrogate the penitent, without inadvertently teaching them new sins by his choice of questions. (According to Tentler, "it seems hardly possible," to exaggerate the significance of the emphasis on confessional completeness. It constitutes the "essential difference" between Roman Catholic penance and the more general Protestant variation [Tentler, 1977: 91–101].) Following confession, penance proper is prescribed as a "remedy against infirmity." The therapeutic element is emphasized. With skills acquired from previous clinical "practice," the priestly "surgeon" sensitively, but diligently, examines the "patient," inquiring both into their past habits and their present circumstances. Then, after diagnosing the patient's condition they "pour wine and oil" on the wound, using as a basis for treatment observations of outcomes from past "experiments to save the sick."

There is, naturally, a good bit of controversy concerning the frequency with which commoners actually availed themselves of confession. Given the shortage of priests with legal authority to absolve sins, and the notorious clerical practice of extorting "voluntary gifts" from penitents—sizes negotiable beforehand—together with a human reluctance to display one's depravity before strangers, Tentler concludes that yearly confession was probably the rule for the typical believer until the fifteenth century (Tentler, 1977: 70–73, 78–79, 87–88). But he concedes that it was always attended to when the penitent was feared to be close to death, prior to major feast days, or when one wished to receive the Eucharist, a practice rarer in the medieval era than it is today (74). For their part, the penitential handbooks recommend that confession be made as often as conscience demands or as opportunity avails, including daily confession if possible. However, there is no consensus on this. In any case, mere frequency of participation in a religious ritual is not necessarily the best measure of its psychological significance.

Perhaps a more telling index of the salience of confession are the countless references to it in lay literature: Chaucer's "Parson's Tale" (composed ca. 1386–98), for example (Patterson, 1978); Dante's *Divine Comedy* (1313–20), in which seven of the ten divisions of the Mountain of Purgatory are given to purging the seven deadly sins, each represented by a notorious historical figure (Alighieri, 1958: 79–113); the *Confessio Amantis*, authored by Chaucer's colleague, John Gower (1327–1408), consisting of a dialogue between himself and an imaginary spiritual director, illustrating each of the seven sins with examples taken directly from various penitential handbooks (Gower, 1963); *The Book of Margery Kempe* (1436), a fictionally embellished biography of a mystic's struggle to attain the unitive life, in which the heroine (who flourished ca. 1290) does "shrift" two to three times daily and finds herself accused of still another sin, false humility (Butler-Dowdon, 1944); and William Langland's *Vision of Piers Plowman*, the quest of Will and Conscience for Christian perfection, in which the adventurers' journeys are allegorized to the three steps of sacramental penance: the House of Contrition, the Castle of Confession, and the House of Penitence (Robertson and Huppe, 1951). (In this and other pieces, including several of Shakespeare's plays, rapacious priest-wolves are depicted as preying on sly, but largely defenseless, fox-laymen.) This itemization says nothing about the emphasis placed on regular confession in period manuals on home economics: Walter of Henley's *Husbandry*, Robert Grosseteste's *Rules* (Lamond, 1890), or above all, *The Goodman of Paris* (1340). In the latter, care of the household is explicitly associated with care of one's soul, and this with regular confession to a spiritual "surgeon" to whom "wounded men from day to day show their sores . . . to gain speedy and fresh healing" (Power, 1928: 62).

What this all means is that the influence of the penitential legislation of the Fourth Lateran Council was hardly limited to ecclesiastical circles. On the contrary, through its ceremonial procedures, as well as through the moral dictates it enforced, confession deeply touched the medieval imagination. The consequences for commercial record-keeping, to say nothing of politics, military affairs, and sexuality, were immense. Let us consider how this was so.

CHAPTER 3

The "Scrupulous Disease"

Moral Scrupulosity

Soon after confessional penance was made compulsory, reports began to be sounded about a peculiar neurosis (as it would be called today) exhibiting itself among the laity. By the end of the thirteenth century, the occasional reports had exploded into an "epidemic" (Delumeau, 1990: 1): Moral scrupulosity—an overly exacting, paralyzing anxiety; a dread that even an off-hand word, thought, or deed might, if undivulged to the priest, be the one that occasions eternal damnation. (The term comes from *scrupulus*, the smallest unit of Roman measurement [ca. 1/24 oz.].) The scrupulous soul kept meticulous records of their morally suspect acts that they insisted on confessing weekly, if not daily, in an increasingly frantic effort to escape God's censure. The stated goal of the enterprise, of course, was to avoid plunging at death into the fiery maw of Hell; its consequence was sometimes to cripple the penitent's ability to function effectively in an ambiguous moral world.

Although as we shall soon see, scrupulosity by other names was well-known long prior to his time, the official labeling of the condition is credited to St. Alphonsus of Liguori (1696–1787). His characterization still provides the basis for contemporary discussion. "(Scrupulosity is unrestrained apprehension) seeing evil where there is no evil, mortal sin where there is no mortal sin, and obligations where there are no obligations" (Alphonsus, 1905: II, book 1, chap. 2). To this day, scrupulosity remains one of the most formidable challenges for the Catholic pastor; a small library has emerged to explain it and to recommend solutions (Haering, 1963; Lasko, 1949; Lord and O'Boyle, 1932; Ciarrocchi, 1995; Santa, 1999).

23

A number of Catholic pastoral psychologists account for scrupulosity by means of neo-Freudian concepts, arguing that it is the consequence of an overactive superego, perhaps resulting from "fixation" at the so-called Oedipal stage of psychosexual development. Implicit in this theory is the conviction that obsession is a general symptomology, of which scrupulosity is merely an accidental attribute. Were the patient not Catholic, their obsessions would not disappear; they would merely attach to another object.

In his own analysis of the subject, Bernard Haering argues that with its devotion to hairsplitting technicalities, scrupulosity (like its priestly variation, casuistry) evinces all the signs of a "mass neurosis" in that it involves "legalistic fixation" and a "helpless compulsive drive for spiritual security and certainty" (Haering, 1963: 162–63). However, he fails to acknowledge the possibility that confession itself inadvertently might aggravate the condition. My suspicion, independently supported by the exhaustive research of Jean Delumeau (1990: 296–303), is that by forcing penitents' attention away from concrete behaviors (with discrete spatial and temporal limits) onto the unplumbed depths of their inner worlds, confession probably entices more than a few—specifically, those, as it would be said today, without firm "ego boundaries"—off the precarious ledge of moral security into the chasm of vertiginous subjectivity.

As Delumeau shows, long before confession was made compulsory, there was already widespread conviction among Christians concerning the fallen-ness of earth and of earthlings. By the end of the first millennium, an entire literature of *contemptus mundi* had evolved to describe it (Delumeau, 1990: 9–17). Furthermore, a panoply of malevolent spirits were routinely cited to prove it. In addition to this, a cottage industry of magic had been devised to avert their powers: para-liturgical chants and blessings, set-apart precincts, and equipment: holy water, the Virgin's tears, the blood, hair, and body parts of deceased saints, sacred shrouds, and the like (Kaebler, 1998: 101–25). What confession effected was the *psychologizing* of contempt. Penitents were made to understand that decrepitude did not just reside "out there" in the world; it inhabited the deepest crevices of their own bodies, manifesting itself as blasphemous, wicked thoughts and cravings. Each Christian was now positioned to experience themselves as "a demon clothed in flesh" (to quote a period metaphor), as "a devil incarnate," or as a "sewer of iniquity," whose "sins outnumber the hairs on [their] head" (Delumeau, 1990: 1). By means of confession, in other words, fear in the abstract transmogrified into fear of one's *self*.[1]

Whatever its causes, the epidemic of scrupulosity after 1300 calls into serious question the validity of Weber's judgmental stereotype, alluded to in chapter 1, in which the medieval Roman Catholic laity lived "ethically, so to speak, from hand to mouth" in an emotionally impulsive, easygoing, if episodically guilty, accommodation to the world. According to his wife Marianne, Weber was accustomed to contrast this "average" ethic" to the "heroic ethic" of the Calvinist whose life is "a titanic struggle for perfection in the exertion of his own powers," "a fight to the death, . . . between 'God' and 'the devil'" (Marianne Weber, 1975: 155, 306, 322, 323, 364; cf. Oakes, 1988–89: 84–87). The data before us here suggests that the so-called *Protestant* Ethic in fact was flourishing in Europe centuries prior to the advent of Protestantism itself.[2]

To be fair, Weber does acknowledge that some pre-Reformation Catholics conducted moral bookkeeping of the sort later endorsed by Protestant theologians. However, he dismisses the Catholic practice as having had an entirely different motive than that of "the conscientious Puritan," who sought to "feel his own pulse with its aid." The Catholic, Weber insists, tabulated moral accounts merely to "serve the purpose of completeness of . . . confession, or [to give] the *directeur de l'ame* a basis for his authoritarian guidance of the Christian (mostly female)" (Max Weber, 1958: 124).[3] I hope the discussion so far and that to follow, both in this chapter and in chapter 4, unsettles this picture.

જાજ

Scrupulosity, by other names, was showing itself among clerics as early as the fifth century. John Cassian, the Syrian monk mentioned in chapter 2 as having played a preeminent role in the introduction of confession to the West, seems to have encouraged it. "We should," he urged his fellows, "constantly search all the inner chambers of our hearts . . . with the closest investigations lest . . . some beast" furtively insinuate itself "into the secret recesses of the heart." Just as the miller meticulously examines the quality of grain before admitting it to the store, says Cassian, each believer in an effort to rid themselves of their own noxiousness, must scrutinize their untoward desires and thoughts, enumerate them in writing, and divulge them daily to the abbot (Paden, 1988: 69–72).

Bernard of Clairvaux (1090–1153), having witnessed firsthand the paralyzing effects of trying to follow Cassian's advice, criticizes it for promoting *simulata confessio*, "exaggerated guilt," in his *Steps of Humility* (Bernard, 1964: 216–20). In his own penitential handbook (composed ca. 1175), Alain de Lille follows suit, soothing the overly precise conscience of his fellow monks with these words: "But he ought not always to descend to minutiae, . . . for truly a searching after the unknown can give occasion for sin because he who blows his nose too much brings forth blood" (Haering, 1963: 162–63). Raymund de Pennafort (1175–1275) agrees. Being overly zealous in displaying one's infirmities to the spiritual physician, he says, "is not speaking the truth." Rather, it is "admitting falsely for the sake of humility." "As Augustine says, 'if it was not a sin before confession, it is now'" (Bryan and Dempster, 1958).

Both Alain and Raymund insist that while omitting no mortal sin, confession must nevertheless exclude acts that the penitent themselves does not know for certain are sinful. Church doctrine, however, has by no means been clear on this point. In the same paragraph where he cautions against false humility, Raymund warns against a confession that is too general. For while one can comprehend sin in general by confessing particulars, the opposite is not true. Indeed, as early as the seventh century, Gregory the Great was declaring, "it is a mark of good souls . . . to recognize a fault where there is none" (Ignatius, 1964: 137). St. Donatus (who flourished ca. 592–651 CE) was even more insistent: "Confession must be always rendered assiduously and with unceasing zeal, alike of thought, of the idle word, every hour, every moment. . . . Accordingly not even little matters of thought are to be neglected from confession, because it is written, 'he who neglects little things, falls little by little'" (Watkins, 1920: II, 621, 619). (Even the contemporary moral theologian, Haering, admits that scrupulosity can be "a critical stage in . . . religious growth.")

Pope Benedict XI in 1303 enjoined the confession of venial (minor) sins as a "great benefit" (Denzinger,1957: 188, sec. 470). Although this was abrogated by the Council of Vienne eight years later, the Church continued to hold that it is better to err on the side of caution by confessing too much, than failing to be absolved for minor misdeeds and "not enter the gate of Life." The Council of Trent (1551), responding to the scathing attack on confession by one of Christian history's most notable obsessive-compulsives, Martin Luther, upheld this recommendation.[4] Venial sins, the bishops concluded, may be safely "passed over in silence." However, they added, "the practice of pious persons" suggests that they can be confessed rightfully and profitably" (Denzinger, 1957: 275–76, sec. 899). This is hardly less than an admonition to scrupulosity for those wishing their piety to be officially acknowledged.

Thomas Tentler cites some commentators (among them, Antonino of Florence and Jean Gerson) who warned that "if a scrupulous man were to confess all those things that have been written for confessions, he well might keep a confessor in his purse" (Tentler, 1977: 114). But he adds that such caveats are rare (115–16, 156–62). Already by the time of Alain de Lille, some handbooks were urging that penitents keep written records of their sins, their companions in vice, their addresses, and their occupations, all as mnemonic aids in preparing full confessions. Later manuals would recommend that penitents actually bring notes with them to their interrogations (Tentler, 1977: 86; Zimmerman, 1971: 124). This, although Pope Leo X (1513–15) warned against the danger of reciting "individual sins written in little books." It is but a short distance from simple counts of wrongdoing to the finely sculpted, self-abasing confessional autobiographies of the medieval period: those authored by Julian of Norwich (1343–1413?), for example, and Catherine of Siena (1347–1380).

Confession and Accounting

As the personal account of their spiritual development was to the medieval poet and mystic, the financial account was to their more worldly counterparts, the urban merchant and the rural estate manager. In fact, a popular allegory used in period literature to depict the sacrament of confession was precisely that of a "wicked steward" giving an "account" of his misdeeds to the "bailiff" of the manor who serves as agent for the divine "Auditor."

> But thou must abide in the house of thy heart pondering well and examining all thy faults of which thou shall yield account and answer to God and to his bailiff (that is, thy father-confessor). And thou shall think also on thyself, as does he that is required to yield account of his receipts and of his dispenses to his lord. Wherefore every man and woman shall ponder his sins straight-forwardly and look well to the stirrup of his conscience, so that it does not fail in the count. For even if thou fails at thy account, God will not fail at His when he cometh. (Francis, 1968 [1942]: 173–74, my translation)

Today, of course, business records are comprised largely of figures and dates. This is a far cry from the spiritual autobiographies of a Francesco Petrarch or a Margery Kempe. It is therefore difficult to appreciate that originally there might have been something more than just a figurative parallel between business chronicling and moral confession. As an aid in this effort, I offer the following points.

First of all, like biographical accounts generally, medieval business ledgers originally were not transcribed in tabular form, but as complex sentences. Indeed, guild statutes of the day expressly forbade bookkeepers from using Arabic notation and columnar displays in posting accounts for fear that they could too easily be falsified (Raymond de Roover, 1943: 150).[5] According to Armando Sapori, "not a few of the surviving [medieval account] books . . . are so remarkable for beauty and aptness of expression, for acuteness of observation, and for their wealth of information that they have been published for their value as philological texts" (Sapori, 1953: 56). In sum, then, the use or the non-use of numbers and columns by themselves bear little on the purposes served by an account. Business records can be preserved in convoluted longhand; moral ledgers (as the cases of Cotton Mather and Benjamin Franklin, to name just two, demonstrate) can be tabulated and quantified (Sombart, 1967: 117–20).

Second, it also helps to keep in mind that like any action—sex, politicking, or war-making—commerce is an inherently moral enterprise, even if it is not always strictly ethical. In other words, buying and selling are not just mindless movements or "operants" (as Skinnerian psychologists might say); they are conscious acts, behaviors made "meaningful" by the reasons, stories, or accounts given for and about them (Arrington and Francis, 1993). This being so, commerce naturally and easily fell under the jurisdiction of the medieval Church's confessional regime. And as this occurred, business narratives began assuming an apologetic, justificatory voice; to the point that the information reported in them eventually came to comport exactly to that routinely solicited by priests in the course of their confessional inquiries: Who took part in the transaction? What goods or services were involved? Where did it take place? When? Why? And how much money was involved? I will return to the significance of this fact later.

Third and finally. Perhaps not unexpectedly, then, after 1300 a species of moral obsession regarding private business dealings began to make an appearance within the merchant class. This is reflected in the increasingly shrill insistence on the part of period commentators that merchants and bankers keep tidy and comprehensive daybooks and ledgers, in which they "note day by day and hour by hour even the minutiae of transactions . . . never spar[ing] pen and ink" (Raymond and Lopez, 1955: 376–77). It is in this context that the moral—psychological significance of double-entry bookkeeping is best understood.

CHAPTER 4

Business Scruples

Medieval Double-entry Bookkeeping

Double-entry bookkeeping (DEB) first appeared in several Italian cities simultaneously (Raymond de Roover, 1955; Florence de Roover, 1956; Chatfield, 1974: 13–16). Its first documented use is in the Massari accounts of Genoa (Melis, 1950: 527). (These may be anticipated by fragments from the secret books *[libro segreti]* kept by the Florentine banking family of Alberti, to hide papal debtors [Raymond de Roover, 1955; Florence de Roover, 1956].) The Massari books—so named after the word for city treasury officials—date from 1327 when, according to its devisors, a new system was introduced "after the mode of banks," perhaps to avert fraud. At the time, the municipality of Genoa was speculating in pepper, sugar, silk, and wax.

Over the next two centuries, the procedure was disseminated to northern European trade centers. The vehicle that is said to have "launched the future" was publication of the first textbook on DEB, *Particularis de Computis et Scripturis* in 1494. Authored by the Franciscan friar and mathematician, Luca Pacioli (1445–1517), it was one of the first books ever printed on the Gutenberg press and, behind the Bible, one of the most influential.[1] Indeed, the invention of movable type and the popularity of the "Italian method" were probably linked. Printing visually demonstrated how business records could be tidily aligned in bilateral format and concisely quantified, and how different kinds of accounts—cash, expenses, liabilities, assets, and so forth—could be distinguished. In short, printing promoted the kind of thinking that DEB exemplifies (Thompson, 1991; Mills, 1994). While today accounting usually is performed by electronic computer, five hundred years after its publication, *Particularis de Computis et Scripturis* still describes its basic procedures. It was modernity's first calculative technology.

To decipher the motives that might have occasioned the emergence of DEB, it is necessary at the outset to assess first how it was used. I will be brief. As ancient Sumerian clay tablets and (what we know of them) Roman business records clearly demonstrate, permanent, complicated partnerships in credit, trade, and real estate can be conducted successfully without DEB. In fact, according to Basil Yamey, "it is probable that the vast majority of enterprises used a simple form of record-keeping (which may conveniently be called 'single-entry') until well into the nineteenth century . . ." (Yamey, 1949: 105). Even immense corporations like the Dutch East India Company, the Sun Fire Insurance Office of London (1701–1960), the Whitin Machine Company, and the Capital and Counties Bank of England (until 1918) posted their accounts in single-entry (1964: 126). The implication of this is obvious: The popular argument that the "explosive" business climate of late medieval Italy somehow "demanded," "necessitated," "pressured," or was "ripe for" DEB (Littleton, 1933: 15; Mills, 1994: 83, 89; Bryer, 1993)—is far from a sufficient explanation for its appearance, however accurate it may be in other respects. Even less convincing is the notion that DEB is "rooted in the nature of things" (Raymond de Roover, 1955: 45; Chatfield, 1974: 32–43).[2]

Second and more to the point, Yamey argues that while DEB definitely can be used to draw up periodic profit/loss reports by which businesses can then rationally adjust their behavior, evidently it was rarely used for this purpose until long after its introduction. What this implies is that the claim that DEB was "eagerly adopted" because its "superiority as a management tool was quickly recognized" is highly suspect at best. Instead, as evidenced by the instructions contained in early bookkeeping texts, the act of posting each transaction twice in the ledger, as a credit to one account and as a debit to another, was superseded by other considerations: "Firstly [to quote an early German textbook] so that the balances of all the . . . accounts may be conveniently reviewed at once; *and secondly and chiefly, to prove that the books have been kept with accuracy*" (Yamey, 1949: 110, my italics).

Neither the *bilancio del libro* (the book balance) nor the *summa summarum* (known today as the trial balance [Pera-gallo,1956]), which Pacioli extols as the two essential book-keeping operations, have little purpose other than to certify the accuracy of business records. The *bilancio* tests to make sure that ledger postings comport with their corresponding journal entries. (Pacioli provides elaborate procedures to guarantee that this is the case [Pacioli, 1963: 91–92].) The second proce-dure, the *summa summarum* (literally, sum of sums), compares the total credits with the total debits in the ledger itself, to reas-sure the bookkeeper that no errors have been made in it. Luca Pacioli considers this the pivotal accounting operation. If the two totals do not equate to the penny, then a mistake has been made either in arithmetic or in the postings themselves. Such errors "must be searched out diligently with the intellectual ability God has given you" (98).

The *bilancio del libro* and the *summa summarum* were to be undertaken whenever a ledger was about to be "closed," and its open accounts transferred to a new ledger, not as is done today, according to a periodic schedule. While "in the best known places," says Pacioli (Pacioli, 1963: 91), closings are done annually and while this can serve to "maintain lasting friend-ships" among business partners (87), the main reason he gives for closing a ledger is when there is no space in it for additional postings. (Subsequent commentators would later add two other conditions: when the owner ceased business or when he himself died [Winjum, 1970: 750, 751, 760; Yamey, 1949: 104].) Pacioli never directly states that the drawing of balances is undertaken to enable owners to calculate profits so that they can rationally adjust their affairs to market conditions or to determine the investors' shares of the firm's equity. Instead, the "ordering process" involved in ledger-closing "was considered more impor-tant . . . than the income figure which resulted from it" (Win-jum,1970: 750). (James Winjum goes on to agree with Yamey that this was the case with most companies until around 1840.)

This is not to say that matters of profit/loss and capital are overlooked in early bookkeeping texts. On the contrary, one of the advertised features of DEB from the beginning was that it enabled owners to get an overall view of their estate at a single glance and to "reform their measures of living" accordingly (Winjum, 1970: 746–47; Yamey, 1949: 101–2). Pacioli, for example, explicitly acknowledges that "some people keep an account called Income and Expense" from which they assess their profits and losses (Pacioli, 1963: 80). At one point, he even prays that "God may protect each of us who is really a good Christian from" financial losses (97). Nevertheless, it is clear that for Pacioli assessments of profit/loss and capital are secondary to the major object of bookkeeping which, to repeat myself, is to relate the story of the firm's dealings meticulously, thoroughly, and accurately. Nor is this the case for just Pacioli. The terms that he and other period authors use to describe the postings from which profit/loss is determined underscore its marginality. Consisting of a "hotchpotch" of such items as money received from dowries, gambling winnings (and losses), and household expenses, they are variously dismissed as "chaff," "refuse and dregs," and "fictitious." In short, they are items cast into "a convenient receptacle" with others that have no where else to go (Winjum, 1970: 750; Yamey, 1949: 107, 109). The "real," "pertinent," "essential" accounts are those that are about to be transferred to the new ledger (Pacioli, 1963: 80, 96).[3] To say it once more, then, until late in the eighteenth century at the earliest, the most important objective of bookkeeping was not to aid partnerships to maximize profit or to calculate capital. It was instead, says Winjum, to satisfy an "obsession" by bookkeepers with precision and comprehensiveness for themselves.

Alberti, Pacioli, and Datini

What might have occasioned such an obsession? Or, if one prefers a less psychiatric vocabulary: What lay behind a shift in business orientation toward what Werner Sombart calls

Rechenhaftikeit (arithmetic reckoning), a quality so clearly exemplified by DEB?

Without getting into the convoluted history of Western science, a clue is provided by sociologist Benjamin Nelson in the following homey adage: numbers don't lie (Nelson, 1981: 152–63). Although cynics might doubt it, numbers are less easily fabricated than the tongue's slippery words. Having a universal character, furthermore, their meanings can be deciphered by anyone of any culture trained to read them, requiring no special, charismatic gifts. Numbers are more reliable than the intuitive conjectures of theologians and the personal revelations of prophets; more trustworthy than the probabilistic conjectures of moral casuists who hear the confessions of bewildered penitents.[4] "Probabilities of perplexed and doubtful consciences [therefore] give way to [numbers] which have the appearance of precision and which . . . offer . . . mathematically certain demonstrations of the need for one or another policy" (250). As applied to the issue before us, arithmetically precise bookkeeping promised objective certitude in the face of the subjective risks and uncertainties of late medieval commerce.

The penitent's circumstantially detailed, quantified moral ledger aided them to represent their life to their confessors according to a simple yet thorough narrative, and helped them trace their moral progress or regress, if not by the week at least annually. Just so, as a "kind of Ariadne's silken thread [DEB] Conducts [merchants] through the Labyrinths of trade . . . like Theseus it doth devour confusion that monstrous minotaure" (Colinson, 1638: forward): "the confusion of Babel" wherein the merchant's mind "has no rest" and is "always troubled" (cf. Pacioli, 1963: 26; Sapori, 1953: 55–56; Raymond and Lopez, 1955: 376–77; Origo, 1957: 98, 113; Yamey, 1949: 102–3). "For what is a man when his accounts are all in confusion," asks an early advocate of DEB, "but like a ship in a boisterous sea without mast or rudder, which cannot be expected but to sink or run aground. But if accounts be kept regular, there will be a great safety and satisfaction therein" (Winjum, 1970: 745).

Insistence on the necessity of arithmetically chronicling the affairs of one's household and firm, "to the point of bad taste" (to quote one critic), is no where more evident than in the cases of Pacioli, Leon Battista Alberti, and Francesco Datini, three Tuscan luminaries. Each in their own way contributed to the idea, taken for granted today, that the entire universe—including the movements of planets, architectural structures, human physiology, and business reality—is best represented by mathematics.

ജ

The most celebrated of the three, Alberti (1404–72), was the last scion of the renown Florentine banking family of that name: philosopher, architect, musician, and sculptor. His views on numerical record-keeping are important not because they are uncharacteristically extreme for his time—they are not—but because of the intimate relationship with and influence he appears to have had on Pacioli.[5]

To Alberti, business records are never to be dismissed as profane throwaways. On the contrary, "it is almost as if they [are] sacred or religious objects" (Alberti, 1971: 218). As such, diligence and solicitousness in their care "is as acceptable to God" as frequent prayer and daily attendance at Mass. Nor is the registering of one's business affairs something to be done when spare time allows or is farmed out to underlings for the sake of more important tasks. Instead, Alberti believes that the merchant has no less than an ethical "duty . . . to write everything down [himself] . . . and to check everything so often that it seems he is always with pen in hand" (205). "I should often want to examine and verify even the smallest matters," he once boasted, "at times even inquiring about things already known to us, so that I should seem more diligent. . . . Benedetto Alberti used to say that the Merchant should always have his fingers stained with ink" (205).

It is a revealing comment on his fastidiousness that Alberti appears sensitive to charges that his advice smacks of something not completely healthy. Cognizant that he has, perhaps, waxed too eloquently enthusiastic on these matters, he cautions readers that conscientiousness should not go so far as "seeing if the lamps have too thick a wick. . . ." Tasks like these, he suggests, are best left to women (Alberti, 1971: 215–16).

Like his mentor, Pacioli also lauds the virtues of wakefulness, sobriety, and industry. In *Particularis de Computis et Scripturis*, he writes that the good manager is now here, now there; sometimes in the shop, sometimes at the market, and at still other times with the owner at fairs, while the shop is left in the hands of women "who can scarcely write" (Pacioli, 1963: 34). Alert as the rooster who keeps nightly vigils in all seasons without rest, he has "a hundred eyes" to oversee his enterprise. "Yet [even] these are not enough for all [he has] to say or do" (33). To facilitate vigilance and to clear his mind of less important matters, the manager should therefore keep memorandums, journals, and ledgers that are clear, complete, and cross-referenced.

Pacioli is not content to justify his advice by promising greater profits to those who follow it, any more than Alberti is. Profit is mentioned only occasionally, and then primarily as an aside in the course of his discussion of the *summa summarum*. Instead, vigilance and the bookkeeping that enables it, constitute nothing less than cardinal virtues, ends in themselves. "In the divine offices of the Holy Church, they sing that God promised a crown to the watchful" (Pacioli, 1963: 34). The sine qua non of good business, Pacioli argues, is the habit of arranging one's affairs in a "systematic way," which is to say, with mathematical proficiency (25–26). Risk-taking and long-range planning are nowhere mentioned.

The reader may object that neither Alberti nor Pacioli are representative of the average Italian businessperson of their times and that it is unfair to generalize from their outlook to that of the typical merchant. Both men were unusually gifted and refined humanists. Pacioli, for example, was an acclaimed professor of mathematics and a friend to the younger Leonardo da Vinci. For his part, Alberti's sculptures and buildings are still looked upon as signal examples of Renaissance art. This objection could be sustained, then, were it not for the writings of a far less perceptive wool merchant whose dispositions toward record-keeping are even more fanatic than Alberti's or Pacioli's: Francesco di Marco Datini (1335–1400) a man who "epitomizes" Tuscan character, according to his biographer (Origo, 1957: xvi).

According to Iris Origo, Datini suffered from the malady par excellence of the early modern burgher, angst: a sense that his little world, built from personal labor, was perpetually on the verge of catastrophe. Using Alphonsus of Liguori's characterization of the condition (cited in chapter 3), we can easily diagnose his state as one of moral scrupulosity. For like the scrupulous personality generally, Datini sensed perils everywhere and trusted no one, including his own slave wench (Origo, 1957: 116, 117, 123, 144). Indeed, he claimed to be less wary of the devil himself than of his business competitors upon whom he unconsciously projected his own larcenous inclinations.

Fearing misfortune at every turn (Origo, 1957: 130–35, 137, 138, 139)—once even dreaming of his house collapsing in pieces (136)—Pacioli tried to ward off disaster fetishistically (as Freudians might say), by compulsively committing every banal detail of his affairs to writing. So much so, that the Datini archives—for he likewise insisted that every scrap of parchment be kept in perpetuity—comprise the greatest treasure of private medieval memorabilia in existence: 150,000 pieces of correspondence, 500 account books (in double-entry), 300 deeds, and hundreds of other instruments.

Datini corresponded with his wife, Magherita, and with his peasants and agents daily. None of them were permitted to act without his written consent: "veritable Bibles," Origo calls these memorandums. "No detail was too small to deserve his notice," including, if we may believe Magherita, the very length of the household candle wicks. "No omission or extravagance [was] slight enough to escape his reproof" (Origo, 1957: 98, 382). So meticulous are the Datini records that we know the price of a child's cymbal in fifteenth-century Florence, the price per rod of every bit of cloth in his wife's dowry, the cost of a tailor's services, and even of a handful of peacock feathers. We can also observe how, like other favorably situated citizens, Datini tried to circumvent Florence's sumptuary laws, enacted to avert a negative cash flow to the Orient.

Datini's obsession with the written word, not surprisingly, alarmed his business partners, his spouse, and his own physician, all of whom worried about the dangers of self-induced physical debilitation. Surely, says Magherita, you must be weary of tormenting yourself with your nightly watch (Origo, 1957: 236–39). After collapsing from nervous exhaustion in 1395, Datini admitted as much: "I am not feeling very well today, on account of all the writing I have done in these last two days; without sleeping either by night or day, and in these two days eating but one loaf" (185–86, 352). Alas, even after coming to realize that his was a little more than a "dog's life" wherein he was frantically driven "like an old horse in harness," Datini was no more able to temper his demons than the modern obsessive-compulsive is, continually at the sink, futilely washing away imagined dirt and pollution (97, 159–61).

I hesitate to attribute Datini's condition to the sacrament of penance alone. Few psychological ailments are reducible to a single factor. In any case, like many Tuscan merchants, Datini was not naturally pious. But this caveat should be viewed from the perspective of an era when the Church had immeasurably more hold over the European psyche than it does today. In fact, Datini met all the devotional obligations of a person of his rank and then some, including providing alms to pilgrims and the sick, donating liberal tithes to the Church, fasting, attending Lenten sermons (which he particularly enjoyed), and making frequent confessions. Twice in 1399 he undertook penitential pilgrimages barefoot and garbed as a beggar (Origo, 1957: 356–65). Another time, sick and near death, he ordered five Franciscan brothers to his bedside to hear his final confession. During the height of the Plague in 1400, homilies on the Final Judgment preached by his personal spiritual director convinced Datini to give his entire estate to the destitute lest, at the final audit, "the Creditor would demand of you an interest too heavy to bear" (309). For wisely following this advice, Datini is remembered today in his hometown of Prato as "The Merchant of God's Poor" (241, 368, 384–86).

In short, what we witness in the case of Datini, and in a more muted way with Pacioli and Alberti, are some of the very qualities of the capitalist spirit enumerated by Weber: sobriety, deliberation, the "avoidance of sleep and sloth" (Alberti), and above all vigilant record-keeping. To be sure, we are still some distance from Weber's full-blown inner-worldly ascetic who not only labored like a monk, but abjured as well the "idolatries" of fancy dress, erotic music, dance, rich foods, intoxicants, and theater (Weber, 1958: 168–75). This would have to await the arrival of the Puritan divines.

Final Observations

Business chronicling and penitential confession both were expressions of a late medieval project in moral improvement. Each involved the "casting of accounts," the first to an auditor; the second to the Auditor (God). This is not to say that sacramental confession "caused" the upsurge of business accounting after 1200, at least in a mechanical way. Nevertheless, it definitely provided the model for it, down to the kinds of information bookkeepers were urged to write down. More importantly, with its focus on intentionality, its recommendation that penitent's examine their consciences daily, and its requirement that it be circumstantially detailed and numbered, confession had the following unintended consequence: It encouraged merchants, already so inclined, to begin recording every aspect of their transactions day-by-day and hour-by-hour; and not just once, but twice, so as to guarantee their impeccability. What this suggests is that Sombart's and Weber's equation of numerical calculability with rationality, is probably overstated. For far from being a simple index of rationality, the medieval propensity for numerical chronicling has a somewhat neurotic flavor. While it would be going too far to see it as a conventionally acceptable form of madness, it was certainly a fetishistic gesture intended to gain solid footing in an increasingly unstable world, a fact that I return to in chapter 5.

This is to not to deny that there were perfectly sound financial reasons for keeping accurate books during the late medieval period. Benedetto Cotrugli once cautioned that unless he is like the Persian emperor Cyrus, "who could call every person by name in his entire army," one should never transact business by heart (Raymond and Lopez, 1955: 375). Carefully kept books could serve as a memory aid for international bankers moving credit in several currencies to scores of clients; it could help resolve lawsuits between partners nonviolently; and it could lower the temptation to commit embezzlement by company agents. Hildebrand Veckinhusen (1365–1426), a Hanseatic trader, was cast into prison and died soon after his release when he was unable to redeem the debts accrued by his dishonest employees (Florence de Roover, 1956: 167–68). Yet financial utility alone does little to explain the invention, much less the ensuing popularity, of complex bookkeeping operations. After all, even DEB is no guarantee against financial calamity. Tommaso Portinari, a branch manager for the Medici's (which kept its books in double-entry), was responsible for bankrupting the entire enterprise by extending imprudent loans to extravagant spenders and by his own unauthorized investments in galleys and residences. He was saved from Veckinhusen's fate only by virtue of his status as a diplomat. Hans Memgling's triptych, "The Last Judgement," pictures Portinari sitting naked and smug in the scales of divine justice held by Michael the Archangel (Raymond de Roover, 1963: 338–57).

More to the point, financial considerations do not explain the Tuscan predilection for meticulous record-keeping in areas other than business: in public statistics, for example (Burckhardt, 1928: 76–78), in unpublished private diaries and published autobiographical confessions (Landucci, 1927; Martines, 1967; Zimmerman, 1971), and in the family scrapbooks and *ricordanzi* of the era (Kent, 1977; Jones, 1956; Stern, 1971). The latter registered not only the marriages, deaths, and births (legitimate and otherwise) of both the main and collateral lines of the clan; they reviewed the career histories of its prominent members, recounted its feuds and scandals, and itemized its expenses and receipts, sometimes in grammatical structures identical to those of period business accounts, sometimes in double-entry. It is these and related documents that enable us to distinguish the spirit of this age and place from what went before and elsewhere.

Elements of this literary corpus were authored by men like Datini, who were compelled to keep their fingers ink-stained by demons they could barely understand. Other, more insightful, observers (like, say, Cotrugli, Alberti, and Pacioli) wished in addition to mimic the imagined lifestyle of the Roman patrician. Alberti had read Cicero's orations on Roscius and Verres; he knew that ancient Roman gentlemen who failed to dutifully record their credits and debits could be legally compromised.[6]

But this does not explain why Tuscan merchant-scriviners copied the Romans in this respect and not in others, emphasized even more by Cicero. I believe that the late medieval Italian propensity for scrupulous bookkeeping is best grasped by situating it within the moral atmosphere of the day, an atmosphere partly fostered by the Church's agency of moral pedagogy, the sacrament of penance.

We know that even the most hardheaded medieval businesspeople, perhaps disinclined to avail themselves of other Church ceremonies, nonetheless sought out the consoling words of penitential absolution, *ego de absolvo* (I [in the name of God] absolve you). This is indicated both by papal directives that forbade priests from tormenting penitents about their credit practices, if such inquiries risked causing them to lose faith (Denzinger, 1957: 401–2, secs. 1609–10), and by the baroque casuistry that accumulated like a precipitant around the problematic of commerce after 1300. Let us examine this precipitant more closely.

CHAPTER 5

Medieval Morality and Business

Homo Mercator vix aut numquam potest Deo placere

In the medieval life-world, commerce was morally questionable. As this Latin aphorism by Gratian reads: "Seldom or never can a man who is a merchant be pleasing to God." Mercury (Gr.: Hermes), the deity whose name supplies the root for the vocabulary of commerce—merchant, market, merchandise, and mercer—was also known as the patron of theft. Even in our era, the problematic association between larceny and commerce persists in the words "mercenary" and "mercurial."

In Hugo of St. Victor's discussion of the "servile" or less worthy arts, commerce is spoken of as a "peculiar kind of rhetoric" (Hugo, 1961: 76). For success in selling depends on a skilled tongue and mental acuity that anticipates objections and soothes concerns. To employ a distinction coined by sociologist Erving Goffman, business acumen rests less on concrete skill than on eloquence. It is concerned more with tactical expressive maneuvering and the fostering of appearances, than it is with truth. It is not surprising, then, that in Dante's *Divine Comedy* the merchant is represented by Geryon, "that loathsome counterfeit of fraud," who has the outward features of kindliness, mildness, and honesty, but is fashioned with a serpent's body, the tail of a scorpion, and the rapacious claws of a four-footed beast. Geryon perches on the cliff wall, high above the bottomless abyss of hell (Alighieri,1958: "Inferno," canto 17, 28–30).

It is true that mercy, another of Mercury's children, the quality of the wise judge, has a positive moral resonance. Without mercy, justice is merely an excuse for vengeance and cruelty. But it is also the case that mercy without justice is the

43

mother of dissolution. For mercy is gratuitous gain; gain unearned and thus, strictly speaking, undeserved. If mercy is not tempered then trust, the precondition of social order, is undermined.

Commerce is consistently maligned in medieval moral theology.[1] The Church never objects to truly earned gain, wealth used for public benefit, or fortune that does not upset the presumed "divinely ordained" hierarchy of estates. Her concern is always with "avarice," the second in order of deadliness of the seven mortal sins: gain that is excessive and not fairly labored for. Of the different species of avarice, that which monopolizes the attention of moralists is usury, an act which, to use the contemporary medieval phrase, first steals and then sells back what belongs to God alone: time.

In his *Decretum*, the first and one of the most influential compendia of Church laws (1159), Gratian in an uncanny anticipation of Karl Marx distinguishes between the "worker," who buys either to use or to refashion a thing for sale (and who for these reasons is without blemish) and the "merchant," who buys only to exchange for a higher price later. All merchants are evil, says Gratian, and "cast forth from God's temple" (Tawney, 1948: 34–35). But the most insidious are usurers, for they profit even as they sleep. Indeed, far from working for their money, money works for them.

From this distinction Church lawyers would derive others that are met with increasing frequency from the twelfth century on, and that culminate in the decrees of the Council of Vienne (1311): There is out and out usurious "theft" versus honest "rent" charged for the use of one's property; there is "notorious" usury (which is confirmed by several witnesses) and "occult," secret, usury. Finally, there is the distinction between "certain" usury, where the victim is known by name, and "uncertain" usury, where the victim remains anonymous. The bottom line: He who charges unfair interest or extorts excessive charges for goods with full awareness of what he is doing, is an outlaw. As such, he is subject to interdiction, refused absolution, denied a Church burial, and condemned to eternal damnation. This, unless he makes formal restitution for civil damages either to the wronged party or to the Church in their behalf (Noonan Jr., 1957: 15; Denzinger, 1957: 149, sec. 365; Nelson, 1947).

The scholastic proscriptions against usury had three sources: Deuternomic injunctions against charging interest on loans to fellow Jews (Deut., 15.7–10; Lev., 25.35–37), the subsequent theological glosses on these, and the ancient Roman legal restrictions on interest-taking, updated in Charlemagne's legal code. Some authorities maintain that both the Hebraic and the Roman prohibitions originated from military considerations. Imprisonment of, or revenge on, a clan brother or a fellow legionnaire for not paying interest on credit extended to him could compromise the organizational discipline and fighting prowess of the army. In place of interest, then, the obligation of mutual aid to clan brothers arose, with the implicit promise of recompense in-kind. Under Christianity, the notion of brotherhood was universalized; not taking interest became a duty of the faithful (Weber, 1950: 267–68).

However this may be, usury never was considered simply a sin against brotherly love. Instead, like theft, it is a crime against justice because it takes from another what is rightfully theirs (Noonan Jr., 1957: 30–33). To say it differently, in usury (as in robbery) one gains without returning something of equal value to the victim. Thus, it is unearned gain. Or, insofar as Catholic moral theology locates sin in the intention, it is the *hope* of gaining financially through lending. The standard Thomistic argument goes like this: People may rightfully profit on qualities "intrinsic" to the goods being sold. Because the values of commodities such as animals, wheat, and slaves vary (due to of changes in the demand for them, or because of differences in their sizes, strengths, or yields), then prices for these may also rightfully vary. Money, however, is intrinsically a medium of exchange and nothing more. To charge varying prices for it therefore violates its essential nature (Noonan Jr., 1957: 52). Like the sin of sodomy, this is *contra naturam*.

Ancillary arguments were composed to amplify this argument. For example, interest takes another's labor unfairly because only the debtor is truly at risk with a loan; or, money bears no fruit and thus its use should have no price; or again, money should be used only to purchase things for consumption, not to earn more money; or still again, a loan is a transfer of ownership, thus no usage fee on it is permitted (51–70, 73–79). Whatever the argument, any person who participates in usury is, in the words of Bernardino of Siena, "worthy of eternal death." "Accordingly, all the saints and all the angels of paradise cry then against [the usurer] saying, 'To Hell, to Hell, to Hell.' Also the Heavens with their stars cry out, saying 'To the fire, to the fire, to the fire.' The planets also clamor, 'To the depths, to the depths, to the depths'" (77).

The Franciscan ideal of poverty profoundly impacted generations of believers after 1300. The struggle between the Franciscan Conventualists and the Spritirualists over the permissibility of private property was not just an internal debate; it engrossed the entire society. Evangelical lay orders such as the Tertiaries and the Fraticelli, who denounced material riches flourished, even in the merchant class in Florence. Francesco Datini, the conscience-besieged wool merchant introduced in chapter 4, was a lay-Franciscan brother.

In the eleventh canto of "Paradiso" Dante Alighieri, one of Florence's greatest sons, celebrates St. Francis's "marriage" to Poverty, "a widow for eleven hundred years," and until his time "un-wooed." Only Francis's life is capable of keeping the ship of Peter on course, says Dante. He who follows Francis's example "will load himself with priceless merchandise." But now Peter's flock hungers for "strange food" (i.e., money). So great is their "gluttony" that they are found "scattered in many pastures growing rank," returning to the fold with empty udders. Included with the barren sheep are Dante's countrymen, Catello Gianfigliazza, and the patriarchs of the Ubriacchi and Becchi families. *The Divine Comedy* pictures them burning in the lower levels of hell, weighed down by their purses that hang like millstones from their necks (Alighieri, 1958: "Inferno," cantos 17 and 28–30).

Already in 1265, three generations before Dante's time, another Florentine, the popular encyclopedist, Brunetto Latini, would prove that material fortune is a danger to happiness.

Instead of citing Church authorities, however, he cites the pagan pundits Cicero, Seneca, Horace, and Juvenal. "Good fortune is blind, and so may blind us in turn," Latini argues. "The one who hastens to increase his wealth often loses his virtue," and with it his reputation. For it is of the nature of material riches that they increase the appetite of their owner for more, tempting them to theft. "Money wants you to be its slave." Therefore, if you truly wish to be free, diminish your covetousness. As Juvenal teaches, "Nothing is more noble, nor honest than to despise money" (Latini,1948: 296–99). Later humanists would go even further, claiming that because poverty is the basis of virtue (manliness and power), then it must have been the ultimate source of ancient Roman Imperium. Alas, what Romulus founded in poverty, the emperors Sulla, Marius, Pompey, and Caesar destroyed through greed and dissipation (Baron, 1938: 15–17).

Medieval Commerce

The full significance of the Church directives against usury and commerce can not be understood out of context of the way in which the great fortunes of the thirteenth and fourteenth centuries were garnered. For as every student agrees, Church law did little to hinder the development of business (Noonan Jr., 1957: 101–15). Usury could always be taken from those outside the brotherhood of Christ—Jews and Muslims—without mortal danger, and from those considered to be holding illegal benefices. Following Roman legal precedent, furthermore, profits on loans could be entered into ledgers as "gifts" or as "rent" for the temporary use of the creditor's resources (Ehrenberg, 1928: 43). In fact, the statutes of the Florentine Calimala Guild in 1332 required this (Raymond de Roover, 1963: 11). Mountains of Piety, as they were known, money brokerage firms, established by civil authorities to solicit capital for loans to the poor (in exchange for a small fixed interest rate) were expressly allowed even by the most conservative casuists (Denzinger, 1957: 238, sec. 739; Noonan Jr., 1957: 295–310). (It is a comment on the legitimacy of Montes that the Franciscans founded their own, at first charging nothing, then later, at the urging of St. Bernardino, insisting on a nominal fee. This fueled a dispute between themselves and the Dominicans, who pretended to be scandalized by the compromise.) Again, citing Roman civil law, Church jurists found it easy to justify creditors charging "late fees" and "fines" on loans not redeemed in time, or on the difference yet to be repaid. A handful of innovative casuists went so far as to defend the idea that profit opportunities forgone *(lucrum cessans)* and financial losses incurred through money-lending *(damnum emergens)*, created entitlements to interest charges.

A close examination of medieval trade reveals that many important credit transactions did not involve the fixing of interest; hence, they escaped Church purview altogether. Several of these were based on the ancient Roman law of partnership (Max Weber, 2003: 54). There was the *commenda*, for example, in which one party supplied all the capital for a trading venture to a second party, who sailed with the goods to market. Two-thirds of the profit went to the investor, the remainder to his agent, providing effortless gain for the former and a means to a quick fortune for the adventurous man without means. Comparable arrangements were the *societas maris* and the *compagnia di terra* (63, 67, 75; Florence de Roover, 1956: 86–90; Noonan Jr., 1957: 133–35, 143–45, 149–52).

The most creative way to circumvent Church law was the international money exchange: a testimony to the shrewdness of the Tuscan mind (Usher, 1943: 77–90; Raymond de Roover, 1944). This permitted transfers of funds, de facto loans, from Florentine merchants (in florins) to their agents in Bruges or London, where they were converted to francs or pounds. The transfer was done by a written bank warrant (*cambium per litteris* = exchange by letter), not through the physical movement of coin. Because there was a greater demand for Florentine luxury items in France and England during the thirteenth and fourteenth centuries than for French or English wheat or wool in Italy, florins were worth far more in Bruges or London than they were in Italy. As a result Florentine merchants were virtually assured of making anywhere from 8% to 30% profits on their "loans" (Raymond de Roover, 1963: 117–22). These were duly entered into ledgers not as prohibited interest-earnings, but as permissible gains due to differences in money value between countries, arising from variations in supply and demand (1944: 386–94; Pacioli, 1963: 76–79).

With some exceptions, Church casuists remained skeptical of *cambia per littera* until long after the Reformation. This, because they were seen to contradict the Thomistic thesis of money's "intrinsic" nature as a neutral medium of exchange (Noonan Jr., 1957, 118–31, 311–23). Likewise, loose variations on the procedure: they too were considered anathema and deserving of excommunication. Included among them were "dry" exchanges, so-called because there was no actual purchase of foreign currency; "fictitious" loans that hid the identities of creditors by means of false names; and interest-bearing loans for which there was no written record. Pope Pius V (1571) expressed the Church's position in these words:

> [W]e condemn all those exchanges which are called fictitious (elsewhere, dry), and are so devised that the contracting parties at certain market places . . . pretend to solemnize exchanges, at which places those who receive money, actually hand over their letters of exchange, but they are not sent, or they are so sent that, when the time has passed they are brought back void, whence they had set out; or, even when no letters of this kind were handed over, the money is finally demanded with interest, where the contract had been solemnized. (Denzinger, 1957: 311, sec. 1081)

The Troubled Conscience

Max Weber insists that during the medieval era "a business career was possible only for those who were lax in their ethical thinking" (Weber, 1963: 220; cf. Pirenne, 1937: 28–29). He bases his claim on the "astounding cynicism" of guild statutes that protected members from being summoned to Church courts on charges of usury or, if they were found guilty, of providing lump-sum payments to ecclesiastical authorities in their behalf. Such devices, says Weber, "created an effect of mockery of Church law" (Weber, 1954: 253, 54, n. 114). Surely, he exaggerates. According to Benjamin Nelson, Christ's counsel to the rich young man made a "profound impression" on many late medieval businesspeople (Math 19: 16–26; Mark 10: 17–27). The diaries and family *ricordanzi* of even the most avaricious Florentine merchants reveal that many of them undertook gymnastic efforts to avoid colliding with Church law while still making a profit, or of making "spectacular" restitutions involving hundreds of beneficiaries when this failed (Nelson, 1947: 113–14). Meanwhile, "hundreds of other leading families," proud of never having transgressed laws against usury, nonetheless voluntarily donated "vast sums" to underwrite debtor's prisons, chapels, convents, and hospitals; and not on their deathbeds, but at the very heights of their careers (115, 118–21). Consider once more the case of Francesco Datini.

In 1398, Datini proposed to his partners that they enter the lucrative banking industry. The partners responded fretfully, warning him that to become a loan-maker would imperil both his reputation and his soul. This, by associating him with "Lombards" (a pejorative term of the day, standing for any Christian usurer) and Jews. "For there is not one of them who practices no usury" (Origo, 1957: 153). When Datini went ahead with his plans anyway, undertaking a series of dry exchanges, one of the partners quit the firm out of fear that the king of Aragon would try him for theft. As for the notary who wrote up the contracts, he pleaded with Datini to make restitution for his crimes, adding, "I think I, too, should confess and make penance" (154). Two years later, Datini saw the error of his ways. He immediately ordered his Barcelona agents to desist from making further loans. This allowed him to brag belatedly to his wife that he had never made an illicit profit (158–59).

During an age when family honor was considered the sine qua non of manly honor *(virtù)*, few devout sons of wealthy magnates had the audacity to act as Francis of Assisi, who renounced his father's textile firm and became an itinerant monk. On the contrary, countless otherwise perfectly ethical young men, burdened with a sense of family obligation, reluctantly entered the world of commerce. Think of Giovanni Boccaccio, Francesco Petrarch, Bracciolini Poggio, Giannozzo Manetti, Donato Acciauoli, and Niccolo Niccoli. All six of these men began their adult lives by dutifully following the business paths set out for them by their merchant-fathers, each harboring grave doubts about their decision.

Manetti was a deeply devoted Catholic and distinguished Hebrew scholar. Yet he ended up serving as his father's bookkeeper. Boccaccio's father actually tried to set his son up in business in Paris. The enterprise failed after the son developed a passion for poetry while studying bookkeeping. Marsilio Ficino was able to garner the gumption to leave the commercial world only after his father died. Likewise, Niccolo Niccoli. Francesco Petrarch would likely have made a career out of bookkeeping had it not been for his father's untimely death. Bereft of any financial patrimony, he was freed to pursue his calling as a poet, a career he pursued (by his own admission) with mercenary ambition. Pandolfo Rucellai actually labored as an exchange banker before becoming a Dominican brother (a denouncer of usury, and ultimately a saint), which he was able to do only after being widowed and enfeebled by old age. Acciauoli, son of a Florentine banker and part owner of a silk workshop himself, volunteered restitution for the profits he realized through exploitation. Known "far and wide" for his moral scruples, he even indemnified the friars of Certosa for the failure of his ancestors to recompense *their* sins. The stories are virtually endless.[2] Any notion we might harbor that medieval merchants typically were ethical Neanderthals who ignored Church law with impunity or skirted it without experiencing moral squeamishness is, simply, incorrect (Ehrenberg, 1928: 43; Noonan Jr., 1957: 3; Raymond de Roover, 1963: 12; Pellicani, 1989: 64–66). As late as the sixteenth century, businesspeople were still anxiously asking their spiritual advisers whether specific undertakings were legally permissible. When John Eck, an apologist for the Fugger family, then serving as papal bankers, issued a judgment that lenders may licitly make profits even when they neither labor nor risk their capital, merchants of the period were "jubilant," according to John Noonan Jr. (1957: 208–9, 212–17). The family subsequently financed his visit to Bologna, the center of canonic learning, to argue his case. Benjamin Nelson sums up the realities of the situation this way:

> Although it is not possible to show that very many financial magnates succumbed to the ravages of an evil conscience . . . their number and their eminence are sufficient to indicate that . . . the purse strings of "capitalism" were [not] . . . secure against the claims of a hallowed, still compelling morality and religion. (Nelson, 1947: 114)

Closing Remarks

Conscience is a vague intimation that a disembodied other monitors one's innermost thoughts and yearnings. Sociologists consider it the internalized voice of parent, priest, preacher, or public. The price for not heeding one's conscience is guilt, shame, self-doubt, and what psychoanalyst, Theodor Reik, has identified as *Gestandnizwang*, a compulsion to verbalize one's iniquity to an authority (Reik, 1959: 193–211). This, in order to experience the catharsis of self-revelatory abasement (and subsequent forgiveness). In addition to this, at least for superstitious natures, confession also can be used symbolically to avert personal calamity, premonitions of which are often induced by guilt.[3] And during the late medieval period, nothing was more predictable than financial misfortune. By 1350 Florence's original 80 banks had shrunk to 57; within a few decades more, the number was down to 33. By 1490 there were not enough registered members of the banking guild to fill its offices. Similar trends are observable in Venice and Bruges (Raymond de Roover, 1963: 16).

The first exchange bank for which there is record, the Leccacorvo Company of Genoa, went out of business in 1259 because its customers failed to remit their loans (Lopez, 1979: 13–18, 20–23). The Knights of the Templars, who had their own banking business, met an even worse fate: Philip the Fair, their major debtor, dissolved the order in 1321 to maintain his own solvency. He then confiscated its French assets and prosecuted the Knights for practicing satanism. Jacques Coeur, still another lender, was contracted during the Hundred Years War (1337–1453) to raise money for the French. When they reneged on their obligations, Coeur was financially destroyed. To support his own adventures in the same conflict the British monarch, Edward III, indebted himself to the Bardi and Peruzzi families of Italy. When he refused to repay what he owed, most Florentine banks collapsed with them. (One of the major risks of extending credit to princes or to Church officials was that they might justify their refusal to repay on grounds that their creditors had infracted the laws of usury. Few creditors could go to the same law that they themselves had skirted or broken to obtain satisfaction.)

Of all the major Florentine lending institutions, only those of the Strozzi and the Alberti families survived into the fifteenth century (Jones, 1956: 191–92). Those that came later never attained the size or the power of their predecessors, yet many of them suffered the same end. The most notable of these, the Medici, eventually sank under the weight of credit extended to a number of unreliable profligates such as Charles the Bold and his father-in-law, Edward IV. Established in 1397, the bank lasted for a century, after which the family itself was exiled and its holdings put into receivership (Raymond de Roover, 1963).

The downfalls of the so-called Lombards routinely were accompanied by popular revolts against their agents and families, occasionally culminating in the burning and looting of their *castellas*. After all, it was the masses who in the end were forced to pay the taxes and tithes to maintain the credit-ratings of civic and Church authorities. It did not take great minds to link these burdens with sinful loan-making, this to financial collapse, and both to God's terrible judgment, the Plague.

The upshot of all this is that medieval merchants had very good reasons to "cast up accounts" to the communities that tolerated them and to the Creator, quite apart from any financial payoffs that might accrue to them for doing so. To come clean on the matter of what was already considered a morally compromising activity was insurance—all be it symbolic and illusory—against God's wrath, to say nothing of irate neighbors. No one has said it more directly than Robert Colinson, an early English bookkeeping instructor:

> If [the merchant] be fortunate it [bookkeeping] satisfies the world of his just dealing, and is the fairest and best Apologies of his innocence and honesty to the World, and Contributes exceedingly to the satisfaction of all his friends and well-wishers, and to the Confutation and silencing of all his malevolent and detracting Enemies, and proves the great cause to bring him to a most favourable Composition with his Creditor [namely,God]: whereas those that are ignorant of it, in such a Condition are censured by all, when they have nothing to show but bare words to vindicate themselves. (Colinson, 1638: 1)

Colinson goes on to argue that of all the possible varieties of accounting for one's business dealings, that which is most effective in assuaging private consciences and mollifying public concerns is "the true forme of bookkeeping, according to the Italian methode," which is to say, DEB (double-entry bookkeeping). Who, specifically, devised this "methode?" And how, exactly, did they go about their work? These are the matters of chapters 6 and 7.

CHAPTER 6

The Notary-Bookkeeper

During the late Middle Ages, two outwardly opposed tenden-
cies flourished in the provinces of central Italy: world-rejecting
Franciscan enthusiasm and international banking. This probably is not a coincidence.

By 1340 in Tuscany and Umbria alone, nearly one hundred major credit institutions were extending credit and in
doing so, implicating themselves in "usury of the most dread-
ful sort" (Martin, 1936: 47–53). If not outraged by the situation, many Church-going denizens of the region nonetheless
were deeply offended by what they witnessed, even if they ben-
efited indirectly from it. To express their concern, more than a
few of them took up the cross of Francis of Assisi. That is, they
abandoned material things altogether for a life of chastity, obedience, and poverty. For the far more numerous and less
morally adept citizenry, however, this was asking too much.
They chose instead to remain in the world and to negotiate the
quivering tightrope of Church law without dropping into the
fiery pit. The merchants among them sought to remove doubt
of their rectitude by confessing to (and being absolved from)
their sins by the parish priest. In addition to this, they also
began providing accounts to civic auditors, using the "the true
forme of bookkeeping" to justify their dealings. The prepon-
derance of evidence suggests that this bookkeeping form was
fashioned by public notaries, licensed professionals trained in
the art of composing written documents after pre-set, rhetorically engaging figures. This chapter shows how late medieval
notarizing came to be infused with the theory of ancient
Roman rhetoric. Chapter 7 celebrates the beauty of their work.

ოა

The oldest account fragments, dated 1155 and 1164, consist of
sheets slipped between the pages of a cartulary of a Genoese

notary, Giovanni Scriba (John the Scribe) (Florence de Roover, 1956: 86–90). These detail three partnerships between a sedentary principal and a traveling agent. They attempt to calculate the division of profits (characterized by Giovanni as "tremendous") on a basis proportional to the parties' original investments. The location of the sheets clearly demonstrates that originally, at least, the drawing-up of contracts and the keeping of books were aspects of the same job. Although eventually a division of labor emerged between the drafting of documents and bookkeeping proper, as late as 1494 Luca Pacioli would describe the steps through which owners had to go to have their ledgers certified by notaries so that "they can not so easily lie and defraud" (Pacioli, 1963: 38–39). Pacioli elsewhere mentions one book in particular as having influenced his own ideas about bookkeeping: *Liber Abaci* (1202), by Leonardo Fibonacci, son of the official notary of the colony of Pisan merchants on the Barbary Coast (Taylor, 1956: 76). Fibonacci states that his intent in writing the book was to teach Arabic notation, as used by his father when keeping accounts for his employers.

How is it, then, that notarizing came to be associated with bookkeeping? The story begins in ancient Rome.

Roman Law and Notary

The "genius" of Roman jurisprudence was its emphasis on proper form (Jolowicz and Nicholas, 1972: 199–201). Max Weber uses this fact to explain why the "corpus juris," as he prefers to call it, was "extrinsically rational" (Max Weber, 1954: 61–64) and why it was therefore "one of the most important conditions for the existence . . . of capitalist enterprise" (305). Roman citizens viewed ritual correctness as a kind of "fetish," according to Weber (124–25, 131), which could magically make things out of nothing—including, in the case of the later Roman Catholic Eucharist, the body and blood of Christ out of bread and wine. For all this, nevertheless, the traditional Roman attitude toward the practical efficacy of writing was always skeptical. Until around the second century BCE, civil law recognized only contracts made by the delivery of goods (the prices of which were fixed "by copper and scales"[1]), or those solemnized by ritual exchanges like this: *Spondes?* (Do you engage yourself?) *Spondeo* (I do engage myself). Then, as the tongue has spoken, so shall it be law *(Uti lingua nunc upssit. Ita jus esto)* (Jolowicz and Nicholas, 1972: 279–81; Max Weber,1947: 121, n. 49; Littleton, 1933: 29–30).

To effectively govern its barbarian, non-Latin-speaking subjects during the age of the empire, Roman civil procedure was forced to accept the use of written instruments. Predictably, in order to be considered legally actionable, following the ancient preference for proper style, these too were required to adhere to a recognized question-answer format. As the Justinian Code, a fourth-century compilation of Roman Law, says: "If drawn up by a *tabellio*, it must be formally complete and finished throughout" (Usher, 1943: 40–41). This, naturally, led to a demand for letter writers, or as we know them today, public notaries. Originally, a clean parchment would be ceremonially delivered by one of the contractors to a preappointed location. It would then be written upon in the presence of all concerned. What bound the parties to the agreement was not just the information transposed onto the parchment; it was the correctness of the procedure itself.

After the empire collapsed during the fifth century CE, the art of letter writing atrophied, but it never completely disappeared. In the rural outreaches of the old empire, the making of contracts reverted to ceremonies of oral stipulation, certified by holographs of the hands of the contractors. Legal disputes, in turn, were resolved by torture, combat, and oath-taking. He who passed the test was adjudged the truthful party, not he who documented his claims in writing. In Church courts, on the other hand, and in Frankish and Lombard royal courts, as well as in Italian trade centers, the arts of the notary were preserved largely intact. Here, the signature on the contract referred not to the names of the contractors, but to the official stamp of the correspondent who composed the instrument binding them. The importance of writing increased when, responding to requests by bankers to streamline international trade, Pope Alexander III issued a ruling granting written instruments validity in ecclesiastical courts in 1169. Subsequent independent supporting judgments by various secular courts confirmed this.

One of the first consequences of these decisions was the introduction of the bill of exchange *(cambium per litteris)*, mentioned in chapter 5. This enabled the transfer of credit in one currency (in one country) to another currency (in a second). The lender profited off the differences in the exchange rates between the two locations, while ostensibly evading Church usury laws. With writing now recognized as a contract-making medium, simple ledger postings of the transactions came to constitute prima facie evidence for them. These postings were made by certified notaries. (Today, they are treated as private in-bank communications and entered into the books by company accountants.) Notaries periodically were required to swear self-condemnatory oaths to the accuracy of their ledger postings. The penalty for fraud was excommunication from the notarial guild (Pacioli, 1963: 38–39, 58, 59, 76; Usher, 1943: 11).

A second, more telling, implication of Alexander III's *decretal* was the professionalization of the notarial arts, and with it the acceptance of notaries as a dominant segment of the *popolo grosso* (the fat people or New Rich, as opposed to the Old Rich and the Middle Class) (Max Weber, 1954: 210–11, 278; Usher, 1943: 50–53). Of course, notarizing had always required training, but traditionally notaries had acquired their skills informally, by serving apprenticeships under locally prominent "doctors" of law. Now, the earning of a license necessitated matriculation at an accredited university. By the end of the twelfth century, the University of Bologna was offering classes in Roman legal forms, grammar, rhetoric, and correspondence (known as *artes dictandi*, from *dico* = to report). As these subjects grew in popularity, related specialties began to appear: *ars poetica, ars historia, ars ethica* (secular ethical colloquy, à la Brunetto Latini), and not the least, *ars notaria*: the construction of deeds, wills, contracts, and business chronicles.

The offerings in *artes dictandi* met with such extraordinary success that they quickly spread to cathedral schools
throughout Europe, including Oxford University (ca. 1250).[2]
The influence of Oxford's alumni is traceable in the growing
uniformity and intricacy of writs, conveyances, bonds, and
manorial and borough accounting in late medieval England
(Oschinsky, 1956).

Within a century and a half after the introduction of *artes
dictandi* at Bologna, the technical demands of the notarial arts
had compelled its faculty to establish its own college distinct
from the college of liberal arts. Its graduates already were orga-
nizing themselves into guilds to gain control of the writing market. By 1255 the field could boast of its own textbook, *Summa
Artis Notariae*. It was authored by a university grammarian
who labored part-time as a notary and bookkeeper for the
banker's guild in Bologna (Rashdall, 1936: 97–124).

Roman Law, Rhetoric, and Double-entry Bookkeeping

The rise of notary-bookkeepers is associated with the revival of
Roman Law, as well as with the explosion of commerce in
Europe after 1200 CE. This being so, more than one historian
has been moved to suggest the embryo of DEB (double-entry
bookkeeping), as a quasi-legal procedure, also can be found in
the corpus juris (Smith, 1954; Kats, 1930).

Evidently, however (at least according to the foremost student of the subject), such a conclusion would constitute "a fundamental error" (Ste. Croix, 1956: 19). True, notaries did
"treat the corpus [of Roman Law] as the very law commerce"
(Max Weber, 1954: 210), taking from it not only the concepts
of the *commenda* and the *societas maris* (2003: 63, 67, 75), but
in addition to this, notions like rent, gifts, agency, and the bill
of exchange (Jolowicz and Nicholas, 1972: 282–83).[3] Furthermore, as we saw earlier, patrician Roman families were
required by law to keep daybooks and ledgers. Nevertheless,
the compilations of Roman Law by Justinian and by Gauis,
which were the major sources consulted by medieval notaries

in devising their contracts, provide only the barest outlines of single-entry procedures (Littleton, 1933: 29–35). Even Cicero's letters to Atticus (Cicero, 1953), which were also known to them, and that detail how Roman financial records were used (and abused), contain no hint of DEB. In any case, the issue is largely moot. Roman business records were transcribed onto wax boards; all of them had long since perished by the late medieval period. Indeed, bookkeeping of any sort appears to have disappeared entirely by 500 CE, due to fear by property owners that they might suffer the same fate as Verres, the embezzling Roman governor, whom Cicero helped prosecute, using his own cooked ledgers as evidence against him (Ste. Croix, 1956: 47–48). What this all boils down to is this: The stylistic features of DEB definitely have a Roman pedigree. However, the roots of the technology are not to be found in Roman Law. Instead, they are located in Roman oratory.

The seminal event in the rebirth of Roman rhetoric was the realization by essayists like Alberic of Monte Cassino (ca. 1109) that the arts of persuasion, which heretofore had been restricted to the oral arena—especially, to courtrooms and legislatures—could be adapted to writing. Alberic's *Flowers of Rhetoric* made all the then-known oratorical formulas—generalized to writing—accessible to budding correspondents (Miller, 1973). However it is the notary public, Brunetto Latini, Dante's mentor, who is considered the first great product of the emerging *artes dictandi*. Three-fourths of his widely disseminated *Tresor* is a verbatim translation of Cicero's rhetoric text, *De Inventione*, with suggestions on how to apply it to literature (Latini, 1948; East, 1968: 241–46).

Cicero was acclaimed the unquestioned Master of Eloquence throughout the late Middle Ages (Murphy, 1967). His *De Inventione* was the only rhetoric translated into common vernaculars during this period. This, and Latin versions of his *De Oratore*, his *De Partitione Oratoria*, and the pseudo-Ciceronian *Rhetorica ad Herennium* constituted the fundamental teaching material for the *artes dictandi*. It is from these sourcebooks that the rhetorical plea that would later be acclaimed as the "Italian methode" of bookkeeping was fashioned.

In modern parlance, the noun "rhetoric" is often accompanied by the pejorative qualifier "mere." It stands for florid diction, bombastic demagoguery, and misleading metaphors: in short, of style without substance. It may therefore stretch the reader's credulity to learn that an evidently scientific operation like DEB is fundamentally rhetorical. During the late Middle Ages, however, while science and rhetoric were distinguishable, they were not housed as they are today in the wholly separate precincts of laboratory and stage. More to the point, rhetoric was far from being viewed as ancillary to the major goings-on in society. On the contrary, concerning as it does the art of how to lead—or to use the modern term, "manage" or "administer"—people, the practice of rhetoric was judged the very glue that makes orderly life together possible.

According to Aristotle (whose rhetoric was also available to medieval notaries), this so-called rhetorical glue comes three forms (Aristotle, 1954: II.2). There are ethical appeals (technically known as *ethos*), wherein the speaker (or in our case, writer) seeks to move the audience by invoking his or her own upstanding character; emotional appeals *(pathos)*, by which the writer appeals to the audience's feelings; and rational appeals *(logos)*, in which the writer appeals to their capacity to reason. To say that DEB originally was stylized to maximize its rhetorical impact, then, is far from claiming that it merely played on people's emotions and pretensions, and was therefore unscientific. Rather, it is to assert that DEB is far more than simply an empirical depiction or explanation of business affairs. To paraphrase Aristotle, perhaps it would be preferable were accountants able to influence audiences through inductive and deductive logic alone. But since they cannot, they must also foster the impression that the proprietor whom they represent is sensible and morally decent, and sympathetic to the audience's interests.

Cicero calls the process of reflection on, and preparation of, these rhetorical tactics *inventione*. Having been "invented," they must next be arranged. This, he names *dispositio*. It consists of the several parts to be discussed in chapter 7. Finally, there is the task of eloquently presenting the material *(elocutio)*.

This involves the deployment of ornate words and figures of speech, and the presentation of the argument in an eye-pleasing, sonorous format (Cicero, 1949). Let us see how these three considerations bear on DEB, as seen through the eyes of those who first practiced and taught it.

CHAPTER 7

The Rhetoric of
Double-entry Bookkeeping

The object of this chapter is to show how the major stylistic features of DEB (double-entry bookkeeping), as expounded upon in Luca Pacioli's *Particularis de Computis et Scripturis*, were modeled after the principles of Ciceronian rhetoric. This is not to suggest that the treatments of their respective subjects are identical. While Pacioli does use the Ciceronian categories "Inventory" and "Disposition" to entitle the two major divisions of his treatise, Cicero himself acknowledged that if a dictator (a speaker or writer) were to be persuasive, he or she had to flexibly adjust their appeals to the situation. Medieval professors of *dictamen* typically broke betrothal letters, forensic arguments, homilies, historiographies, poems, and business accounts into the same general parts, but they understood these to be addressed to very different audiences. Hence, it would have been inane for such documents to parallel each other in any but the most general way.

I hope the reader recalls that although Pacioli's was history's first known bookkeeping text, the operations it depicts had been in use for at least a century and a half before his time. In other words, Pacioli may have successfully conveyed DEB, but he did not "invent" it. Who in fact did may never be known.

The Invention of the Ledger

By *inventione*, Cicero means the process through which an orator goes to "discover" his or her argument: the primary sources consulted, the experts interviewed, the things observed, and so on, the *topoi* (Gr.: places) or loci they visit. For Pacioli, the ledger is the final argument that merchants present to the auditor; the journal and the memorandum (the daybook) are the places they go to "invent" their case. This being so, says Pacioli, the "transactions [recorded in them] can never be too clear" (Pacioli, 1963: 40). The complete daybook should contain all the facts necessary and sufficient for defending claims in court, for protecting oneself from litigation, and for resolving disputes among partners concerning a just division of the profits.

Pacioli describes the invention of the ledger as entailing two steps. In the first, the bookkeeper transfers relevant data from the daybook to the journal. When he does this, the daybook's prose sentences are replaced with briefer statements containing technical terms such as "per" and "a," and technical marks like parallel lines. Once having done this, the bookkeeper then posts each journal entry twice into the ledger, as a credit to one account and as a debit to another (Pacioli, 1963: 43–44, 45–47).

Pacioli recommends that the following information be recorded in the daybook or memorandum: the parties to the transaction (distinguishing, of course, between the person to whom something is sold and from whom something is bought), the nature of the goods or service in question, where it took place, its date, the amounts involved, the conditions under which it occurred, and any witnesses to it. "No point should be omitted in the memorandum," including if possible, "everything that was said during the transaction" (Pacioli, 1963: 40).

This information is identical to that routinely sought by period priests during their confessional interrogations of penitents, which underscores the likelihood that both enterprises emerged from comparable circumstances, namely, from popular knowledge about how credible defenses and prosecutions were readied: *quis* (who), *quid* (what), *quare* (where), *quando* (when), *qunatum* (how much), *cum quo* (in whose presence), and *cur* (how). Authorities believe that the ultimate source of this rhetorical septenary was either the so-called Master of Eloquence himself, Cicero, or his student, Victorinius (Cicero, 1949, I.xxiv–xxviii.35–43; Robertson, 1946). It was subse-

TABLE 7.1
**Information to Be Recorded of Each Business Transaction
according to Luca Pacioli**

1. Who? Giovanni Lombroso
2. What? Cash
3. Where? Padua
4. When? 23 Oct. 1348
5. How? As a loan
6. How much? 300 lire
7. Witnesses? Franco Peruzzi

quently mediated to medieval writers through Boethius's discussion of the circumstances considered essential in determining the legal status of courtroom defendants (Leff, 1978). How Italian public notaries received them cannot be determined for certain, except to say that for both medieval Italian schoolboys and college students, primary instruction in composition included rote memorization and drill in the seven questions. As for Pacioli in particular, we know that he studied both the art of letter writing and Ciceronian rhetoric as a youth. Perhaps more to the point, his own personal experiences in confession might have made systematic inquiry into the septenary seem almost second nature. Pacioli was boarded and educated in a Franciscan monastery where weekly, if not daily, confession was the rule.

The Disposition of the Ledger

There is little agreement among ancient rhetoricians concerning the breakdown of the ideal-typical document. Cicero for one divides the forensic argument into six parts (Cicero, 1949: I.xix). The late medieval teachers of *dictamin* reduced this to four and sometimes to three: the *exordium*, the *narratio* (the account proper), and the *peroratio* (the summary and conclusion). I use the tripartite format to organize the following discussion.

Exordium

There is universal consensus among period rhetoricians that a complete composition always must include an *exordium*, consisting of a brief introduction and a salutation. Indeed, from the amount of space devoted to it in textbooks, it appears that the *exordium* is the most important facet of any letter or report. In his *Summa Dictaminis*, Guido Faba (the foremost Bolognese instructor of the art [ca. 1190–1242]) spends eight times more words describing the *exordium* than he does on the three other parts of a document together (Faulhaber, 1974: 95). If an *exordium* is done well, it renders the auditor attentive, docile, and benevolent (Cicero, 1949: I.xv–xviii.20–26; Pseudo-Cicero, 1918: I.iv.7; Cicero, 1942: viii, 28–30).

Exordia are of two sorts. The first is a simple, straightforward introduction. The second is what Cicero calls an *insinuatio*. The latter, he says, should be employed whenever the audience is suspicious of the accountant's intentions (as, e.g., in commerce). "The insinuation," he says, "is an address which by dissimulation and indirection unobtrusively steals into the mind of the auditor" (Cicero, 1949: I.xv–xvi.20–21). He goes on to say that there are several ways to accomplish this. One is to appeal to one's own misfortunes so as to elicit the auditor's pity; another is to misdirect the auditor's attention by pointing out the evil repute of potential detractors; or, one may pander to an audience by "reminding" them of their own virtue, once again putting them off-guard. Finally, the accountant may foster a favorable impression by extolling his or her own modesty and piety. This last is best done by the tactical deployment of "prayers and entreaties with a humble and submissive spirit" (xvi.22). Alberic of Monte Cassino, the first teacher of medieval *dictamin* says it this way. Well-turned insinuations

> turn one's attention from the particular object [being described, say commerce], somehow, by this distraction of attention, [they] make the object seem different, [they]clothe it, so to speak, in a fresh new wedding garment; by so clothing it, [they] sell us on the idea that there is some new nobil-

ity bestowed. And what else can I call it but "selling us," when a man takes an [object] that is petty in its content and heightens it by his treatment so as to convince us that all is new, all delightful." (Alberic, vi.1, in Miller, 1973)

Alberic cautions that too much of a good thing can backfire. Don't, he warns, invoke pious references to such a degree that they become "poppycock." A meal served with color enhances the appetite, but too much frippery can afflict a reader with nausea. Likewise, it might be said by extrapolation, the *exordia* deployed in business records should ask for God's favor, but they should do so sparingly so that the auditor's defenses are not aroused. The rule is subtlety and misdirection.

Without exception, Renaissance ledgers open with the following *exordium: a nome di dio Guadagnio* (in the name of God and Profit); or, with a more elaborate version such as this from the books of the Florentine company of Corbizzi, Birolami, and Corbizzi (1332–57):

In the name of God and of the blessed Virgin Mother Madonna St. Mary, and of St. John the Baptist and the Evangelist and of all the Saints, male and female, of Paradise, that by their holy pity and mercy they will grant us grace for a holy, long, and good life, with growing honor and profit, and the salvation of our spirit and body. (Yamey and Edey, 1974, 143–44, my translation; cf. 145–46; Raymond and Lopez, 1955: 381–407; Geijsbeek, 1914: 95; Raymond de Roover, 1958: 46–48)[1]

Additionally, it is common to find atop each ledger page either an exclamation like *Laude Deo!* (Praise God!), "Christ be with you all," or more typically, a holy cross ("+Jesus, Florence 23 May, 1380"). These literary devices, together with the practice of crediting *Dio* or *messere Domendeddio* with some of the profits—God's so-called credit entry—unequivocally demonstrate that medieval merchants sought to create the impression that profit was not being pursued in an ethical or spiritual vacuum. God himself, Christ's own mother, Mary, and the saints and angels witness not only to the truth of the ledger entries, but more importantly, to the justice of the earnings accrued. Ill-gotten (usurious) gains, as noted in chapter 4, typically are restituted back to victims or to charitable Church trusts set up for them (Raymond and Lopez, 1955: 419–20; Raymond de Roover, 1958: 48; Nelson, 1949: 114–19; Usher, 1943: 77).

Pacioli explains these practices thusly: The object of business may be profit (although as seen earlier, he is never this direct). But the capital required for running a successful firm will not be loaned a merchant unless he has good credit. Among his most precious assets are his trust and fidelity, "[for] truly everyone is saved by faith, without which it is impossible to please [even] God," much less mortal man. "Therefore, [they] should commence their affairs with the Name of God at the beginning of every book, always bearing His holy name in mind," or with "that glorious sign from which all enemies of the spiritual flee" (Pacioli, 1963: 25, 27, 37, 45, 48, 100; Raymond and Lopez, 1955: 376; Geijsbeek, 1914: 95, 109).

The significance of Pacioli's directives is best understood within the context of medieval trade, wherein contract-making was eminently personal. Being, as it was said, of good honor and unblemished reputation *(bonae famae et illesae reputationis)* was, if one hoped to prosper, absolutely essential. Being acknowledged as upright and reliable in turn rested upon successfully conveying an impression of devoutness. A century and a half before Pacioli took up his pen, Paolo da Certaldo in his *Libro di Bouoini Costume* (1350), identified the relationship between business acumen, honesty, and piety in this way: "Persons who fear the Lord can easily save more money than those impious ones who purchase vanities. Disregard of religion leads to economic laxity in oneself and others. Beware of dealings with the . . . man who disregards his soul; such a person will fail to observe good faith in his dealings with you" (McGovern, 1970: 244; Alberti, 1971: 204; Latini, 1948: 304). Benjamin Franklin could not have said it better.[2]

Paolo, of course, was a renown cynic (as, by the way, was Franklin). He could advocate a show of piety in one setting, then with no qualm recommend bribery and chicanery in another, if it suited his purpose. The same cannot be said of Pacioli. His insistence that business always be conducted in "the sweet name of Jesus," has all the hallmarks of sincerity. For profit-seeking to avoid being mere avarice (theft), he believed that it must always be integrated into the Christian cosmos. "Seek ye first the kingdom of God and His righteousness, and all these things [namely, profit] shall be added unto you" (Pacioli, 1963: 34). He even asks the reader to "remember to pray to God for me that I may proceed always doing well to His praise and glory" (98).

To be sure, Pacioli has been criticized for his evident lack of Franciscan-like virtue. This is inferred from the fact that Pope Julius II personally granted him the right to his own private property to a total of 300 large gold ducats in 1508 (Taylor, 1942: 359–60, 365–67, 371). Some historians have even accused him of having plagiarized *Particularis de Computis et Scripturis* from a text then in use at the Venetian school of arithemetic (in his defense, see Yamey, 1967). Without attempting to assess the truth of these charges, it is enough to appreciate that Pacioli was probably no less devoted than other Franciscan Conventuals of his day. (Unlike Franciscan Spiritualists, Conventualists did not renounce private property.) He condemned of the practice of keeping secret books to veil the identities of silent partners in trade; he served as house master for his order twice, in 1504 and 1510; he enjoyed friendships with seven different popes: All of this argues in favor of his "exuberant piety" (Taylor, 1942: 114–25, 198, 367–70).

Narratio

The appeal that the ledger makes as a rhetorical composition is that the business in question is honest and its profits just. How, it might be asked, can a written document lend credence to such claims? At a minimum, by being brief, concise, orderly, lucid, comprehensive, and above all, consonant with reality. Or, in Cicero's words: *brevis, aperta* (clear), and *probabilis* (Cicero, 1949: I.xx.28; Cicero, 1942: ix.31–32; Pseudo-Cicero, 1918: I.ix.14–26). As depicted by Pacioli, DEB meets all of these criteria. The ledger postings are honed of extraneous words and phrases, yet provide information on all seven of the conditions related to each transaction; every technical term and mark has a single, unambiguous meaning; the transactions are posted in chronological order; and painstaking efforts are undertaken to guarantee their accuracy.

Accuracy is accomplished by the following procedures. When each statement from the daybook is transferred to the journal (a shorthand record of each day's dealings), a mark is made across the daybook entry. This prevents it from being mistakenly entered into the journal more than once. There, it is transcribed on the left-hand side of the journal page if it is an obligation owed to the company, and on the right-hand side if it is the company's own obligation. Each journal entry is then transferred to the ledger not just once but twice, as a debit to one account and then as a credit to another. When it is posted as a debit, a vertical line is drawn on the left-hand side of the journal entry. A second line is drawn on the right-hand of the journal entry when it is posted as a credit (Pacioli, 1963: 45, 49–50, 53).

The *bilancio del libro* and the *summa summarum* (the trial balance), both described in chapter 4, provide two additional checks on accuracy. The first tests to see whether the ledger postings equate with their associated journal entries; the second compares the total sums of credits and debits in the ledger itself. In the event that either of these tests fail, the bookkeeper is enjoined to search out energetically the source of the error. When it is found, it must never be erased; this, after all, would cast suspicion on the bookkeeper's honesty and on the repute of the firm. Rather, the nature of the mistake must be noted next to the relevant entry or posting so that the auditor need not stumble across it himself (Pacioli, 1963: 90; Geijsbeek, 1914: 113).

Nor is this all. Pacioli tells the reader that if billing statements are consistent with company records "as far back as the debtor insists on going, . . . he will like you and trust you more" (Pacioli, 1963: 88). Furthermore, no space should be left in the company's journals between the last entry on a page and the first

TABLE 7.2
Hypothetical Medieval Ledger Postings
based on Luca Pacioli's Directions

In the Name of God

+Jesus   MCDIII
On this day, Cash shall give to
Capital CLI lire in the form of
coin.
                    CLI lire
Cr. ref. page

+Jesus   MCDIII
On this day, Capital shall have
from Cash in the form of coin
CLI lire.
                    CLI lire
Dr. ref. page.

+Jesus   MCDLXXX
Giovanni Bessimi shall give, on
This day, CC lire, which he
promised to pay to us at our
pleasure, for the debt which
Lorenzo Vincenti owes us.
                    CC lire
Cr. ref. page

+Jesus   MCDLXXX
Giovanni Bessimi shall have back
on Nov. II, the CC lire, which he
deposited with us in cash.
                    CC lire
Dr. ref. page

+Jesus   MCDLXXIV
On this day, Jewels with a value
DLXX lire, shall give to
Capital.
                    DLXX lire
Cr. ref. page

+Jesus   MCDLXXIV
On this day, Capital shall have of
from Jewels, a value of
DLXX lire.
                    DLXX lire
Dr. ref. page

+Jesus   MCDXXX
On this day, Business Expense
for office material worth CCC lire
Shall give to Cash.
                    CCC lire
Cr. ref. page

+Jesus   MCDXXX
On this day, Cash shall have
from Business Expense CCC
lire.
                    CCC lire
Dr. ref. page

---

on the subsequent page. Instead, he suggests that a line be drawn from the end of the last entry to the beginning of the next. Any gaps would cast doubt on the bookkeeper's rectitude (85–86).

It is worth saying again that Pacioli devised few, if any, of these operations. He merely reiterates what was standard bookkeeping practice of the day, particularly in Venice. Guild statutes of the era already declared that mercantile records be kept in chronological order, and that they contain neither blanks nor erasures. Tearing leaves from a journal was an offense deserving of excommunication from the notary guild. Pacioli himself is cognizant of the dire legal consequences of bookkeeping fraud (Pacioli, 1963: 58).

Peroratio

The *peroratio* is the summary and conclusion of an argument. The *peroratio* of an error-free ledger (and the balance sheet that was its subsequent historical derivative) is this: Since for every credit there is an equal and corresponding debit and for every debit an equal and corresponding credit, therefore the total credits equals the sum of debits; the total debits equals the sum of credits.[3] Or, to express it in ordinary language: We own a particular amount because at some other time we have given (or owe) an equivalent amount. In other words, the conclusion is not simply that such and such is the net worth—the capital— of the firm, but that this worth is morally legitimate. This, because it arises from a fundamentally equitable, balanced series of transactions.

Since Plato, it has been recognized by moral philosophy that justice speaks to balance (Pieper, 1966: 44–109). The classical icon of justice is the blindfolded judge—Dike, Astrea, or Libra—who holds in her left hand the scale that measures weights of good and evil, credits and debits; and in her right, the sword of decisiveness. She sits full-faced in bilateral equilibrium on a throne precisely positioned between two comparably size columns. In astrology, she is the eighth enigma of the tarot, which stands for equity, harmony, and balance.

Recall that the scholastic criticism of usury was not just that interest-taking is selfish or unloving, but that it sins against justice. This, because the lender gains more than he gives. He profits off what is not his to have, namely, time. True, one should rightly be reimbursed for services provided and the costs, if any, of moving currency between locales. Or, as Pacioli says,

TABLE 7.3
Hypothetical Summa Summarum (Trial Balance)
Based Luca Pacioli's Directions

In the Name of God

Lorenzo Brothers
+Jesus Year

	Debits	Credits
Cash	4,100	
Accounts Receivable	5,200	
Office Material	2,200	
Furniture	20,000	
Accounts Payable		2,800
Capital		10,000
Carryover		7,400
Sales		35,000
Wages	13,000	
Rent	3,000	
Taxes	2,500	
Emergency War Levy	2,200	
God's Account	3,000	
	55,200 lire	55,200 lire

"for your ink, paper, rent, trouble, and time you get a just commission, which is always lawful" (Pacioli, 1963: 78). But to earn more than this, by capitalizing on flukish changes in the demand and supply of currency, for example, particularly when no currency actually changes hands (as in a *cambium per litteras*): There is something morally questionable in this. Double-entry bookkeeping destabilizes this critique, even if it does not entirely destroy it. It does this by demonstrating with mathematical precision that for every profit made, an equal (set of) debts has been incurred. Even with loans at interest, justice is served.[4]

Thomas Aquinas distinguished between three kinds of justice: commutative, wherein each party to a sale, for example, is equally satisfied; legal, wherein an individual gives restitution to the community in proportion to the seriousness of his or her crimes; and distributive, wherein shares of the commonwealth are allotted to citizens in ratio to their contributions to it. The ledger validates that the business in question is just in all three senses: It has discharged (or is about to) its obligations to creditors in an amount equal to what it has borrowed; it has paid taxes, levies, tithes, and restitution, discharging its debts to God and commune; it has paid wages proportionally to its employee's labor and reimbursements relative to its stockholders' investments. Other bookkeeping operations may well be as accurate as DEB, but none can offer such a visible and compelling proof of a company's ethicality.[5]

Elocutio

Eloquence is not simply speaking or writing in a grammatically correct way; nor is it merely speaking or writing the truth. Some ways of arranging words, and some word choices, are more aesthetically pleasing than others, and thus have more rhetorical force. Late medieval DEB employed a strikingly powerful metaphoric imagery—the trope or figure of personalism—and a uniquely stirring sentence structure or scheme, known as the periodic sentence. Let us briefly examine each of these features.

Personalism

The medieval ledger attributes moral responsibilities to all components of the business, human or not. This is a far cry from the modern ledger. In the course of six centuries, ledgers have evolved from commentaries on the joint responsibilities of actors toward one another into ethically neutered statistical records of a business's dealings.

The existence of personal-moral terminology in medieval business chronicles owes to the fact that commerce originally involved deals between flesh and blood people. In banking, where DEB was probably first used, these took the form of loans and remittances, deposits and withdrawals. Understandably, then, they were recorded in personalistic, moral terms: "X shall give (must give or ought to give) repayment because he has received from us a loan"; "We shall have (must have or ought to have) repayment because X has been given a loan." When nonhuman accounts in revenue, goods, cash, expenses, and so on were introduced, the practice of personalizing ledger postings was generalized. However, the entries now became metaphoric. To cite a hypothetical case of a business buying goods from Z on credit: "Goods shall give (must give or ought to give) to the proprietor because the proprietor has received them from Z"); "Z shall have (must have or ought to have) the goods from the proprietor because he has been given them." But how, it may be asked, can goods have a "duty" to give anything? Or, how can Z have a "right" to something he has already given the proprietor? For the sake of custom, a fiction was invented, namely, that goods are like persons with agency, rights, and duties (Littleton, 1933: 44–49; Littleton and Zimmerman, 1962: 27–31, 37–39).

When the terms "debitor" (he who owes) and "creditor" (he who trusts) were introduced by British and Dutch writers in the sixteenth and seventeenth centuries, the absurdities of attributing personhood to inanimate objects were compounded. Cash was now referred to as a loyal employee. (In one scenario, Cash is written of as "keeper of the money-chest" who "owes" what is given "him" to the firm, and who "trusts" others to restore what "he" has provided.) Merchandise was said to be a salesperson; Expense, his subordinate; and Profit-Loss, the business manager (Littleton, 1933: 56–61). Simon Stevin, an early seventeenth-century bookkeeping instructor, asked his students to

> Suppose that someone by the name of Peter owed me some money, on account of which he paid me 100 pounds, and I put the money in a cash drawer just as if I gave it the money

for safe keeping. I then say that the cash drawer owes me that money, for which reason (just as if it were a human being) I make it debtor, and Peter, of course, becomes creditor because he reduces his debt to me. (Geijsbeek, 1914: 15)[5]

The Periodic Sentence

The distinguishing visual attribute of DEB is bilateral posting. It is also one of its most persuasive. One possible, if unlikely, source of the structure was ancient Roman bookkeeping practice (Littleton, 1933: 30–31, 35–36). A much more probable basis was classical Latin, whose style medieval notaries self-consciously sought to emulate. This was not the simplistic grammar of priests and lawyers, but that as had not been spoken or written in over a millennium. Preeminent among its exemplars was Cicero. The fundamental feature of his style is the periodic sentence or, less technically, the serial antithesis, a structure that Alberic of Monte Cassino praises for its "beauty, brilliance, and power" (Alberic, vii.5, in Miller, 1973). A periodic sentence consists of two major clauses in partial opposition, but that are composed in a similar form, and that therefore resolve themselves in an audio and/or visual harmony. Or, to say it more simply, it is a short, symmetrical, counterpoised arrangement of words and phrases.

Francesco Petrarch's tension-filled encounter between his ego and superego, Augustine, epitomizes this style; his *Four Dialogues for Scholars* (1967) provides still another example. To paraphrase: I am a scholar; you are a braggart. But I own many books; sad that you've never read them. I love books; as always, you love the wrong things. My books are well-crafted and striking; there are other, more durable things, more beautiful. But I also have many degrees; degrees are for those who have little to show for their efforts. I, after all, am a professor of liberal arts; professors rarely live what they teach, and so forth.

The poets, artists, and mathematicians with whom Pacioli moved did not just imitate Ciceronian style. On the contrary, by cultivating, it came to constitute their cognitive *habitus*. By means of it their very consciousnesses and visual sensibilities were reorganized. Authorities are able to trace the influence of the periodic sentence both in art criticism and in the "antithetical bias," as one observer has called it, of Renaissance painting and architecture (Baxandall, 1971). The compositions of Leon Battista Alberti, Pacioli's mentor, with their integrated dualities, perspectives, and symmetrical balances of shadow, light, and color, testify to the attempt to generalize the criteria of oral eloquence to the visual realm.

As we learned earlier, Pacioli was introduced to Alberti when the latter was at the height of his fame. While teaching at the University of Milan some time later, Pacioli befriended Leonardo da Vinci, who was studying Euclidean geometry. Pacioli was so taken by Leonardo's sketches on bodily movement that he invited him to illustrate his forthcoming book on balance and proportionality, *De Divina Proportione* (Taylor, 1942). In this, the geometry of the body is allegorized in terms of its cosmic significance. By contemplating the body's relations and proportions, says Pacioli, one can indirectly learn about the totality of creation and of its Creator, the divine Geometrician and Architect. Just as the body is a *discordia concurs*, a harmonized diversity, so is the world as a whole. The head (circle) that circumscribes mind and soul, and the torso (square) that figures the body, are the two principal forms without which God could fabricate nothing (Barkan, 1975: 128).

Few accounting historians have acknowledged the place of aesthetics in Pacioli's bookkeeping instruction (but see Chatfield, 1974: 45). By this omission, they have overlooked still another attraction that DEB must have had to those who adopted it, specifically, its beauty. In his theory of architecture, Alberti writes that the ideal building should be modeled after the human body, the microcosm, the highest earthly manifestation of the principal of oppositional harmony. If this goal is met, he says, then observers will be awed by the recognition, the reknowing, of themselves in the building's structure. And if the building is a church, then worshipers will be transported to the height of communion not only with themselves and with their fellows, but with the God who made them after his own likeness and image.

By analogy, the same can be said of the "architecture" of bookkeeping. The most enchanting ledger (and later, balance sheet) style would be that based on the discordant congruencies of our own flesh, which is to say, something on the lines of DEB. It was this, at least partly, which must have recommended it to late medieval merchants, notaries, and surely Pacioli, schooled as they all had been in Ciceronian rhetoric.

I am not claiming that those who designed DEB set out with the explicit intention of duplicating the scheme of serial antithesis. The history of technology is far from being as simple as this. More likely, we have before us unconscious motives and unexamined assumptions concerning the most visibly striking way to post accounts. As the sociology of knowledge has shown elsewhere, theories often find favor in scientific communities not because empirical facts support them, but because of their elegance and simplicity (Kuhn, 1970). If it is true that enterprises that purport to offer only factual accounts of reality select *their* theories on aesthetic grounds, then how much truer this must be of business accounting, which originally made few such claims: a phenomenon that instead constituted a plea to justify a morally suspect activity.

Final Comments

The previous discussion has by no means exhausted the rhetorical features of DEB as it was originally taught and employed. One that has not been mentioned was the rule that bookkeepers employ Roman numerals "for the sake of beauty" (Pacioli, 1963: 51); another is the convention that credits be posted as close as possible in ledgers to their corresponding debits, because "the nicer it will look" (50).[6] Still another, is the use of repetition of sentence structure. Alberic of Monte Cassino says that of all the stylistic "flowers," repetition is "as splendid as Luicifer who shines more brightly than the heavens" (Alberic v.3, in Miller, 1973). It is a format found in virtually all medieval documents of any importance: private correspondence, legal briefs, bulls, wills, deeds, contracts, and, of course, bookkeeping. Medieval bookkeepers were urged to follow the same pattern again and again in posting accounts, to avoid having them questioned.

In part because of these rhetorical attractions, DEB rapidly spread throughout the Christian world. No competing method could lay claim to making such a favorable impression on an audience; one that had been taught through song, wood block, painting, and ditty that businesspeople are the spawn of Mercurius, the god of unearned gain. In more than a few cases, merchants shared this attitude toward their own calling. If not desperately, then certainly with eagerness, they searched for ways to justify their work, not only to their fellows and to ecclesiastical authorities, but to themselves. Double-entry bookkeeping appears to have answered this need. Developed partly, ironically, through the labor of a brilliant monk of St. Francis, patron of poverty, DEB provided the apology par excellence for the rational pursuit of wealth. Armed with a ready confession in the form of a double-entry ledger, the road to salvation was made a little clearer, a bit less harrowing.

CHAPTER **8**

Confession and Bookkeeping

During the reign of Pope Gregory VII (1073–1085) and continuing into the middle of the thirteenth century, the Roman Catholic Church undertook a far-reaching program to remake the world. Harold Berman considers it Europe's first modern revolution (Berman, 1983: 49–84), the model for all those that would eventually follow: the Lutheran, the Cromwellian, the French, Bolshevik, and Nazi. Like the others, the Papal Revolution was spawned from the loftiest ideals, yet ended in blood: in pilgrimages *(peregrinationes pro Christi)* to extirpate heathen populations and in persecutions of heretics at home (Murphy, 1976). But it also had a softer side. One of these was the introduction of compulsory confession.

During the first Christian millennium, Church doctrine remained largely messianic and socially conservative. Believers were admonished to cultivate indifference to worldly concerns, while eagerly anticipating the Second Coming (Troeltsch, 1960: 39–200). The views of Saint Augustine (354–430), bishop of Hippo and the first angelic teacher of the Church, may be taken as typical. Although the terrestrial kingdom may "sparkle . . . in the splendor of the sun," he writes, and " has beautiful forests populated by admirable beasts," it is for all that material, craven, and "predestined to death" (Augustine, 1972). The celestial kingdom, in contrast, being spiritual is free of sin and is therefore immortal. This being the case, the task of the faithful is not to agonize over the "bitter worries, disorders, afflictions, . . . mad joys, trials, . . . debaucheries, . . . in this sad human life," but to direct their attention to heavenly things.

To promote Augustinian eschatology, monasteries were established throughout Christian civilization: "schools of asceticism," as Lutz Kaelber calls them, modeled after the rigors of the desert fathers of the Middle East (Kaelber, 1998: 62–99). Going by names such as Benedictines, Cistercians, and Cluniacs, each monastic order provided a slightly different path to world renunciation. All of them, however, insisted on poverty, chastity, and obedience. Among the tools used to implement this program of self-mortification were the Celtic penitentials, the handbooks whose contents we examined earlier in chapter 2.

Near the end of the first millennium, theologians began refiguring the received salvation doctrine of the Church. They began to see the world as something more than merely a charnel house to be fled, but as a possible stage whereon humanity might play out its destiny under Church direction (Troeltsch,1960: 201–43). Now, monasteries that once had been given wide latitude to regulate their own internal affairs, were brought under closer Vatican supervision. And whereas earlier, kings and emperors had appointed Church bishops, now they themselves began to be named, judged, and (where necessary) deposed by the Church. There was even a belated effort to enforce "truces of God" on warriors, restricting combat to specific days of the week. A primitive form of international law was entertained, proscribing non-Christian weaponry (e.g., crossbows) and prescribing humane treatment of prisoners. Christian soldiers began to be recast into armed agents in the larger Church project of world renewal: "sinful power to quell sin." Their calling was officially recognized in what the Church honored as an "eighth sacrament."

Nor did medieval Church legislators ignore private affairs. Two mendicant (begging) orders, the Franciscans and the Dominicans, were enlisted to promote the Christian virtues of love and mercy, in place of the ancient tribal customs of honor, vengeance, and heroism (Kaelber, 1998: 80–93). A systematic corpus of legal *decreta*, "Canon Law," was devised; an Office of Penitentiary, a so-called External Forum, was set up to try those suspected of "criminal sins" (Berman, 1983: 185–93); inquisitional procedures were formulated to gather evidence; and an elaborate theory was concocted to "legalize life after death": Purgatory (166–72).

At the End of Time, so it was taught, all the living and dead would be judged. Prior to the Last Days, however, each soul would be brought before a separate tribunal immediately upon their death; there, to give account of their moral debits and credits and to be sentenced to expiate the negative balance. From a Treasury of Merits, a spiritual capital fund amassed through the sacrifices of virgins, martyrs, and saints, the Church claimed the power to shorten the purgatorial sentences of the faithful, in exchange for exemplary behavior. The first "plenary (universal) indulgence" was issued in 1095 by Pope Urban II on the eve of the first Crusade. It promised release from Purgatory altogether if Christ's soldiers were to fall in battle.

In 1215 the distinguished jurist, Pope Innocent III, announced still another forum of discipline, a sacrament equal in binding power to baptism and to the Eucharist: auricular confession. A streamlined variation of the Celtic rite of confession, originally therapeutic and voluntary, now became compulsory and salvific: a hurt *(poena)* that would avenge *(vindicat)* a prior hurt, legally balancing the penitent's moral ledger while allopathically soothing his or her wounds.

Everything was calculated to maximize the reformatory impact of Innocent's penitential rulings. First, unlike the rite of canonical penance that it superseded, there was never any suggestion that confession must or should be celebrated just once after Baptism. On the contrary, as God's mercy knows no bounds, then his ministers could offer "a second plank after shipwreck" to ailing souls, no matter how frequent or detestable their crimes (Denzinger, 1957: 272–73, secs. 894–95). Second, whereas canonical penance had required excommunication, the new sacrament permitted the penitent to continue enjoying the Eucharistic feast even while undergoing his or her cure; which, third, with the introduction of proxies, ransoms (cash substitutes for penances), and mass pardons became decreasingly severe after the thirteenth century (Poschmann, 1964: 211–28). Fourth, if any harbored fear that shameful secrets entrusted to priests might be publicly divulged, this too could be put to rest. By law any priest breaking his vows of confidentiality was threatened with the loss of office and of being "thrust into a strict monastery to do perpetual penance" (Denzinger, 1957: 174, sec. 438).

Berman believes that the Papal Revolution completely altered European society and psychology after 1200 CE. "From a cultural and intellectual perspective, [it] may be viewed as a motive force in the creation of the first European universities, in the emergence of jurisprudence and philosophy as systematic disciplines, in the creation of new literary styles, and in the development of a new social consciousness" (Berman, 1983: 100). The Papal Revolution also effected the modernization of medieval commerce. This, in two ways. First, it provided (an admittedly porous) moral and legal umbrella under which merchants could ply their trade with some security. Second, it inspired the practice of modern bookkeeping, without which capitalism as we know it today would not be possible.

ൟ

Being called to morally account for ones sins to a priest inevitably generalized to "giving shrift" in other settings to different auditors. Or, to say it more precisely, once sacramental confession became routinized into a weekly habit of self-reflection and divulgence, it began to insinuate itself into other realms, serving as a standard for a plethora of accounting practices that appeared in the decades immediately after the Fourth Lateran Council. First came the "little books," as they were called, diaries kept by ordinary penitents to aid them in composing full and accurate confessions; and later, based on these, the secular memoirs of luminaries like Buonaccorso Pitti and Gregoria Dati. Next appeared the systematic confessional autobiographies of the period's mystical adepts: Julian of Norwich, Margery Kempe, Catherine of Siena, and the like. These traced the protagonists' victories against worldly temptation in their efforts to attain mystical union with God. This literary genre of confessional memorializing eventually would assume a more secular form, the classic example being the autobiography of poet Francesco Petrarch, written to his fictive father-confessor,

Augustine. Then came the household *ricordanzi* that accomplished an analogous purpose at a collective level. Composed for the edification of the family's future generations, they didactically followed its moral (and material) progress from mythical origins through a series of epic challenges. Still later came the "political arithmetic" of the city-states of Florence, Genoa, and Venice that Jacob Burckhardt (1928) considers to be the distinguishing documents of Renaissance Italy. And let us not overlook the rural complement to the communal narrative: the manorial account read by the steward to his master, sometimes used as an object lesson on how to confess one's sins to a priest. Finally, there was the confessional reckoning, so to say, which has been my concern in these pages: business accounting.

Profit-making without labor or risk was anathema in medieval canon law. It was a species of avarice (which ranked it second in terms of deadliness of all mortal sins), a crime against justice (hence, a danger to community order), and an act contrary to the theological virtue of charity without which there can be no hope of salvation. Yet, as noted earlier, money-lending at interest not only flourished, it was a primary means by which Italian burghers from the thirteenth through the sixteenth centuries acquired immense fortunes.

One predictable consequence of this evident contradiction was moral anxiety, at least among conscientious merchants. This is obliquely indicated by the extremes they went to alleviate it: restituting ill-gotten gains back to their victims; undertaking penitential pilgrimages; seeking advice from priests on how to avoid sinning while doing business (and failing that, being absolved of their sins through confession); and deploying a vocabulary of commerce that tactfully replaced "interest" and "usury" with euphemisms like "rent," "fees," and "benefits foregone." But the most potent weapon in the merchant-banker's moral arsenal—quite apart from its obvious financial benefits—was DEB. Devised by public notaries who had been trained in classical rhetoric, it helped assimilate the otherwise pernicious work of commerce into the Christian cosmos. It made commerce palatable to the morally squeamish in much the same way that the so-called eighth sacrament of the Church had "Christianized" military violence a century earlier, turning knights from murderers into practitioners of "malicide" (the killing of evil).[1]

As originally conceived, DEB legitimized capitalist accumulation in at least four different ways. First and most visibly, by its deployment of Christian icons and adages, it demonstrated that the Creator himself had a direct interest in the firm as a silent partner of sorts. Buying and selling therefore were perceived as more than just mundane exercises; they were quasi-sacred actions. Second, when the Church was given a share of the profit—via God's so-called credit entry—the Christian character of the enterprise was underscored. Third, DEB required that all deals be entered into journals (and posted in ledgers) as a series of moral obligations and rights. Fourth, and most importantly, DEB proved with mathematical exactness that these sales, purchases, loans, and remittances were honest, balanced, and therefore just.

Sacramental confession bore on medieval bookkeeping not only through its judgments; it also did so through its procedures. By requiring penitents to reflect on the subtlest modulations of their intentions (instead of merely on their outward acts), confession was complicit in fomenting moral fastidiousness in its devotees, including in the hearts of many period merchants, to say nothing of its most outspoken detractor, the great Protestor himself, Martin Luther.[2] Evidence of this is found in the insistence by commentators, "to the point of bad taste," that these merchants use their "ink-stained hands" to record the minutiae of every business encounter; "day by day and hour by hour," including (if possible, said Luca Pacioli) "everything that was said"; and all of this not just once in journals and ledgers, but twice, in order to guarantee their accuracy. Nor is this the end of the story.

More than just an inspiration for modern bookkeeping, confession served as a pivotal "technology" (to borrow Michel Foucault's term) in the social construction of early modern selfhood (Martin, Gutman, and Hutton, 1988). It helped make visible for an entire population, as opposed to a small cloistered elite, the reality of a sovereign, self-referential ego: me. As it emancipated ego from the "collective miasma" of the "we," confession disclosed ego to be sin-inclined and in dire need of clerical policing. Now, instead of serving as a road by which to escape the world (as it had been during the first millennium), penance became a tool by which to reform it. At this moment modern consciousness, with its conviction in the possibility of earthly social progress and self-improvement, was born. One of the documents of its birthing is DEB.

Like confession, DEB empowered some human capacities, reified (made more real) some things, while it disempowered others, rendering them harder to see. Specifically, it liberated the merchant to pursue profits with a clear(er) conscience—this was the boon, as it were. At the same time, it channeled his pursuits into predetermined directions. It did so by compelling that same merchant to attend more and more exclusively to the flow of money through the firm. In doing so, other—in principle equally valid—concerns became marginalized: matters of community solidarity and morality, the mental and physical health of the company's employees, the condition of the natural environment, and so on (Morgan and Willmott, 1993). In the jargon of modern economics, these evolved into "externalities." They became costs (and occasionally benefits) not borne entirely by those responsible for them; hence, not accounted for. Ironically, one of the externalities, one of the unintended consequences, of the introduction of DEB was the enterprise of "accountingzation" itself.

After the effectiveness of DEB as a tool for freeing-up profit-making powers became evident—which, as noted earlier, was a considerable time after its "invention"—comparable calculative technologies were introduced into other "industries": education, government, medicine, policing, agriculture, mining, forestry, fish farming, war-making, and so on. These accounting schemes eventually came to assist the "management" of an extraordinary variety nonhuman and human "resources." Today, the entire planet is well along the path to becoming a gigantic "standing field" (to borrow a

phrase from Martin Heidegger) of "cost-effective utilization."
Each of us is at risk of becoming little more than "a cog in an
ever-moving ['practically unshatterable'] mechanism" (Weber,
1946: 224–30).

Moral Accountability and Business Accounts

I appreciate how, even after all these pages, it still must be difficult for contemporary readers to see how such a prosaic practice like bookkeeping could be religiously rooted and how it
could have had such momentous historical consequences. For
those yet to be convinced, I offer two final illustrations and an
historical musing.

Item one: A series of papal edicts issued during the thirteenth century directing monasteries to centralize their control
of *obedientiaries* (household officials) by, among other things,
keeping written accounts of the community's revenues and
expenses, and having these read annually by Church auditors
(Oschinsky, 1971: 254–57; Cheney, 1931: 443–52).

The first of the Vatican's directives was issued at the very
start of the Papal Revolution by Lucius II in 1144 to the monks
of St. Pancras. These were later reiterated by Alexander III to
the bishop of Worcester. The most notable and the largest vol-
ume, however, are associated with none other than the great
Church reformer himself, Innocent III (Smith, 1951: 92–120).
In Innocent's correspondence on the subject, monastic financial
problems are treated as symptoms of general moral laxity. The
immediate occasion for his directives were reports of simony,
concubinage, violence, drunkenness, and embezzlement. As
these moral plagues spring from the same source and feed on
each other, Innocent reasons, then their cure is to be sought in
the same place, specifically, by more rigorous accountability:
requiring financial audits and personal moral confessions. Both
would be conducted at least once yearly at Easter, hopefully
more often.

The *obedientiaries* railed against Innocent's directives as
"innovations" contrary to divine custom. As a result, they had

to be repeated, first at the Fourth Lateran Council in 1215; then at the Council of Oxford in 1222; at the reformation of the status of the Black Order by Gregory IX in 1238, and finally in Pope Benedict XII's reforms of the Cistercian Order in 1355. Their breach was labeled "proprietarism." It was a crime punishable by loss of the Church's charter, ecclesiastical receivership, and confiscation of monastic land-holdings (Snape, 1926: 66–67). On those estates where the monks surrendered the ancient feudal prerogative to govern their own affairs without external oversight, financial accounting techniques rapidly reached higher levels of sophistication than those on private manors (Stone, 1962). We can also believe that the monk's behavior became, if not less scandalous, at least more canny and discrete.

Item two: Iona community, an ecumenical lay order founded in 1938, is located on an island off Scotland near what was originally a famous monastery (Jacobs and Walker, 2000). It is dedicated to enacting biblically based notions of peace, justice, and individual spiritual growth. Like Pope Innocent III's own reflections on the subject, the Iona communards understand that control over one's receipts and expenses is part and parcel of moral discipline, and that both require the periodic giving of accounts. To this end each member is required to provide written "report cards" on how they dispose of their time and resources, as well as oral confessions. Both are audited by assembled "family groups." Obedience to the Rule is a prerequisite for retaining membership in the community, a status acknowledged by the issuance of a "with us" certificate.

Like the medieval *obedientiaries*, some Ionians have protested against the intrusiveness of these inquiries that remind them of socialist welfare state policies and red tape. A few have even mounted campaigns of civil noncompliance against the presumed outrage; with what effect is still unknown.

Finally, the musing. Today, of course, whatever religious resonances bookkeeping might once have had are entirely gone. Ledger postings have evolved from assertions of a merchant's humility and devoutness into ethically neutered tabulations entirely devoid of religious symbolism. The Cross of the

Crucifixion is nowhere to be seen; the praise to God the Father, once found atop each folio, has disappeared; the dedication of books to Our Mother Mary and to the saints has been forgotten; God's Account has been closed permanently. In short, since the medieval era, accounting has evolved from bookkeeping "fictions," to quote A. C. Littleton, into bookkeeping "facts."

One of the first treatises to fail mentioning the relevance of religious iconography for bookkeeping was Simon Stevin's *Verrechning van Domeine* (1604) (Have, 1956: 243), a text that became the basis of bookkeeping in the Protestant Netherlands, England, and subsequently, America. Because he left no autobiography nor any correspondence, we are left to guess the reasons for Stevin's evident "ignorance" (if that is the correct term) of practices that occupy such a prominent place in Luca Pacioli's textbook, a source from which Stevin copiously borrowed. The following speculation seems reasonable.

Stevin (1548–1620) was probably a Calvinist. This is inferred from his self-imposed exile from the Spanish-controlled (Catholic) Dutch provinces, from the warm reception he received at the University of Leyden (where he was the first to lecture in Dutch instead of Latin), and from his intimate acquaintance with the Calvinist military reformer, Maurice of Nassau (Have, 1956: 241–45).

Now in no other Christian doctrine is the gap between God and the material world so central as in Calvinism (Scribner, 1993). The Catholic tendency, often stereotyped by detractors, to sacralize world affairs so as to render them amenable to the Church's moral guidance—or as Weber would say, to priestly "magic"—was rejected by Calvin as idolatry (Kaelber, 1998: 101–25). Catholicism glorifies the world, while lowering the Creator to the level of his creatures—so, at least, the Calvinist might say—rendering him susceptible to priestly manipulation. Naturally, then, Luca Pacioli's, Domenico Manzoni's, and Do Angela Pietra's insistences that ledgers be opened with the Cross and that business be conducted in the "sweet name of Jesus" likely would be viewed by Calvinists with considerable disgust. According to Calvin, profit-seeking is wholly of this world. Any attempt to dignify it beyond this detracts from humanity's responsibility to attend exclusively to the only proper object of devotion: God in his ethereal transcendence.

In Calvinism worship was purged of worldly trappings: incense, vestments, golden altar pieces, bells, in some cases, songs. This was the intention. Simultaneously, however, the pursuit of worldly things—honor, power, and money—was liberated from spiritual control. This was the unintended consequence. Just as Martin Luther had earlier argued that "holy war" (as in the Crusades) is a contradiction in terms, the Calvinist entrepreneur no longer needed to delude himself that his gains were earned in God's holy name. And just as after Luther, the state was now freed to pursue its power interests without Church supervision, the business endeavors of the Calvinist were liberated from churchly moral encumbrances. Any anxiety that these endeavors might result in the merchant's damnation evaporated. (In Calvinism, man is already damned; nothing he does or fails to do can ever change this. An elite few are predestined for salvation.) Instead, he could pursue his monetary interests with no other concern than the "bottom line."

One of the most telling indexes of Calvin's accommodation to the material world is his treatment of the issue of usury (Nelson, 1949). As pointed out in chapter 5, medieval moral theology based its pronouncements against usury largely on the prohibitions of Leviticus and Deuteronomy. These forbid Jews from charging interest on loans to fellow tribesmen, while permitting it in the case of guest peoples and foreigners. Generalizing from this, the scholastics held that insofar as Christians are one in the "tribe" of Christ, then even converts who are local strangers and one-time foreign barbarians must not be charged interest. Calvin inverted this scholastic principle. True, he argues, in Christ others are indeed our brothers; but it is equally true that just as Cain was Abel's murderer, brothers are also invariably others. Even fellow believers, then, rightfully may be charged usury; so long, of course, as this does not infract commonsense notions of equity and love.

I don't want to exaggerate the departure of Calvin's teachings from tradition. While he endorsed the morality of usury, he also added that it would be preferable were the practice abolished altogether. For one can scarcely profit through inter-est-taking without harming one's "brother." In any case, it must always be avoided in the case of loans to the destitute. Besides, Calvin notes with bitterness, the scholastics have con-ceded so much to the commercial realities of the day that Church law now—that is, by the sixteenth century—essentially prohibits nothing (Noonan Jr., 1957: 365–67).

On this last point, of course, Calvin himself was being hyperbolic. It is true that in a series of decisions between 1822 and 1836—more than two centuries after Calvin—the Roman congregation charged with supervising Catholic morals decreed that interest can be charged; in 1917 Canon Law declared once and for all that interest-taking is licit. Prior to the nineteenth century, however, there remained a profound difference between Catholicism and Protestantism in their attitudes toward usury. The scholastics began with a general prohibition and only later discovered exceptions; Calvinists did the oppo-site (Noonan Jr., 1957: 375–91). The Protestant commentator, Claude Saumaise (1578–1653), went so far as to permit pawn-brokerage to the poor. "Negligence, inertia, or prodigality are the enemies of the poor, not the usurer," he asserts, in words that are disturbingly modern (Noonan Jr., 1957: 371). Not even the most liberal seventeenth- and eighteenth-century scholastics could agree with this.

If it is correct that Catholic Church rulings against usury precipitated doubt and hesitation in the souls of pious mer-chant-bankers, then it is reasonable to suppose that Calvinism's legitimation of interest-taking would have the very opposite effect. This is suggested by the enthusiastic embrace of the Reformed Church by European businesspeople, the fact of which is offered by Weber as confirmation of his Protestant Ethic theory. More to the point, here is the most plausible explanation for the disappearance of pious *exordia*, Crosses, and apologies from Protestant business ledgers. In a word, they were no longer necessary. Stevin's textbook documents an important step in the secularization and ultimately, the demor-alization, of European commerce.

The sacrament of confession, then, may indeed have produced conditions favorable to the introduction of modern accounting (and with it, modern business administration): Werner Sombart is certainly correct on this point. But by disenchanting business altogether, Protestantism probably encouraged it still more. Weber's instincts, if not his specific proofs, are sustained.

Conclusion

The invocation of moral tropes and religious symbols in business records by pre-Reformation bookkeepers and businesspeople was far from an empty mechanical gesture. On the contrary, it was a quasi-liturgical, albeit abbreviated, ceremony; if not a full-fledged sacrament, then at least a sacramental (Kaelber, 1998: 11–12, 114). Through it they were reminded again and again of a truth that might otherwise easily be forgotten in the helter-skelter of everydayness: Everything that one owns is due to God's fortune, the Church's solicitude, and to the community's support, protection, goodwill, patronage, and service (its social capital, as it would be called today). This was more than a recognition that successful businesses accrue debts that must be repaid on pain of committing injustices. Instead, like the realization that without parents one would have no life, it was an awareness of their incalculable, thus nondischargeable obligation to the universe. In other words, it was an awareness of piety (Pieper, 1966). The attitude of pious gratitude has rarely been so tellingly expressed as in these words of the melancholic merchant, Francesco Datini, written when he donated his entire estate to his hometown of Prato: "For the love of God, so as to give back to His Poor what has been received from Him as His gracious gift" (Origo, 1957: 368). There is no rooster-like prating about "self-reliance" in Datini's bequest; nothing is said about his ceaseless labor, pluck, risktaking, and sleepless nights: paeans frequently heard today from the bully pulpits of commerce. There is instead only humility and thanks.

The meaning of piety is not, "I give so that I might have," but "I have so that I might give," and in so giving be redeemed from my guilt, my limitedness, my sins—however it might be enframed: my ontological lack. The man of avarice (in the words of Pope Innocent III) in contrast, "like hell itself, gorges himself . . . without making a return. . . . He is quick to grasp, slow to give . . . [or if he does give] gives only to make a profit, but never makes a profit in order to give" (Lothario, 1969: book 2, secs. xiv and xvi).

Let us admit to a bit of larceny in Datini's heart. In giving back to Prato, it is easy to believe that he was accomplishing his last and greatest purchase, eternal life. Yet, his simple gesture—replicated by countless other merchants of his time and place—was more than this; something closer to a bona fide sacrifice, as sincere and authentic as the offering of any Kwakiutl potlatch master or Trobriand Island gift-giver. For these also give in order to receive later. But more than this, they share their bounty with neighbors, ancestors, and deities in an attempt to alleviate a sense of their own personal insignificance in the face of the bottomless, never-ending Giving that is the universe. All three—the "big power man" of the potlatch, the Trobriand Island cowry shell bestower, and the generous Datini—dramatically acknowledge their stewardship over a benefice that is not finally their own, but is only temporarily given them to manage and answer for.

Appendix

Martin Luther and Scrupulosity

Sometimes the most penetrating insights into the workings of an institution come from those who have consciously disaffiliated themselves from it. Take the case of Martin Luther (1483–1546) and the sacrament of confession.

Luther did not use "scrupulous" to describe his cauterized conscience *(conscientia cauterisata)* (Scheel, 1929: doc. 10, pp. 6–7), but his biographer, Erik Erikson, does: no less than 23 times in the course of 250 sympathetic pages (Erikson, 1958).[1] Whatever term one prefers, Luther was unquestionably conscience stricken (and he had a murderous intolerance of disobedience by others as well). In one place Erikson writes of Luther as being "sensitive"; in another, of his being "precocious"; and in still another, of being simply "negative" or of suffering from a "bad conscience."

Elsewhere, he describes Luther as "autocratic," "tragic," and "overweening." For example, if moderns find it difficult to conceive of any truly *deadly* sins, Luther found it difficult to believe that any were not. He viewed the distinction between venial and mortal wrongs as "particularly impossible," and called the merciful words of Jean Gerson's penitential—"God does not want to demand anything beyond man's power"—a "Jewish, Turkish, and Pelegian trick" (Erikson, 1958: 158; cf. Tentler, 1977: 97). (Luther publicly burned the tolerant and immensely popular penitential handbook authored by Franciscan friar, Angelus de Clavasio, in 1520 [Tentler, 1977: 35].) As a young priest, Luther once felt compelled to confess to having omitted the word *enim* (for) during his consecration of the host. In his mind this picayune oversight was as horrible as parent murder, indolence, or divorce: acts he happily judged the right sins *(die rechten Sunde)* (Erikson, 1958: 144). His spiritual director felt moved to caution him against torturing himself with such trivia (Scheel, 1929: doc. 487, p. 176; cf. doc. 707, p. 276; Erikson, 1958: 156).

It is not certain what occasioned Luther's condition. Catholic apologists sometimes favor the idea of demonic possession; his rival, Erasmus, flippantly attributed it to drunkenness. In Luther's defense, one Lutheran scholar claims that he was an exemplar of Teutonic mysticism. Modern psychoanalysts believe that he was "arrested" at the Oedipal stage of psychosexual development due to his father's brutality. For his part, Erikson considers Luther to have suffered an identity crisis. This small sample from the library of Luther-commentary should serve as ample warning against attempts to interpret the character of such a complex individual by means of a single theory. Nevertheless, it is hard to avoid concluding that Luther's experience with confession aggravated, even if it did not originally cause, his neurotic propensities.

During his formative years, Luther partook in three modes of confession, any of which alone might have been sufficient to produce in sensitive souls like himself a degree of moral obsession. At his Latin school, as in cathedral schools elsewhere, Luther underwent a weekly casting of accounts to the headmaster concerning infractions of the community code, independently confirmed by specially delegated (undercover) class monitors. Delinquent pupils received one caning on the buttocks for each sin recorded in the ledger. "This temporal and relentless accumulation of known, half-known, or unrecognized sins was a sore subject in all of Luther's later life" (Erikson, 1958: 79). Later in the monastery, the equivalent practice was known as *Schuld capitel* (literally, the account of one's major debts). After jointly prostrating themselves in a circle, each monk in turn first acknowledged their own wrongs against the community and then denounced each of the others in these words, "May Brother X remember . . ." (Scheel, 1929: doc. 83, pp. 32–33; Erikson, 1958: 133). As for private non-communal vices, weekly traditional confession was mandated. Here, Luther's scrupulous predilections became fully and absurdly realized.

> In confession . . . he [Luther] was so meticulous in the attempt to be truthful that he spelled out every intention as well as every deed; he splintered relatively acceptable purities into smaller and smaller impurities; he reported temptations in historical sequence, starting back in childhood; and after having confessed for hours, would ask for special appointments in order to correct previous statements. (Erikson, 1958: 155–56; Scheel, 1929: doc. 277, p. 106, doc. 399, p. 146)

So embittered did Luther become toward confession that in the end he excluded it altogether from the Church sacramentary in order to rid her of her so-called whorish Babylonianism (Luther, 1960a: 124). His disgust at commerce in indulgences is already well-known. It is this that struck such a responsive chord with the rebellious German princes and legitimized their secessionist ambitions. However, Luther's critique of penance was more general than this, encompassing the very "tortures," as he called them, of the ceremony itself (Tentler, 1977: 351). These were so exquisite that he once confided to his father-confessor that no word in the Bible is "more bitter to me than 'penitence' " (Luther, 1960b: 66; Scheel, 1929: doc. 812, p. 331).[2]

Racked by "those who . . . teach the so-called method of confession," "distressed by my conscience . . . through endless and insupportable precepts," Luther depicted himself as driven to assume a superhuman work load that resulted in a "poor worn body, . . . terribly weakened and exhausted" (Luther, 1960b: 65, 69–70). Having habituated himself to suspect his own motives, he eventually came to distrust even the feelings of consolation afforded by the words of priestly absolution. These, he became convinced, were still another of the devil's temptations. Desperate from growing awareness that he could never sufficiently atone for the immensity of his evil that confession had led him to sense, even by overfulfilling the satisfactions prescribed by his adviser, Luther undertook a reexamination of the original meaning of the phrase *poenitentiam agite* as it appears in the Vulgate Bible (Matt., 3.2f). Discovering it to be a Latin translation of the Greek *metanoia*, "radical conversion," he came to the insight that authentic penance—freedom from guilt—"only God can grant from Heaven" (Luther, 1960c: 9.1).

Not only had the Church missed the point of penance, Luther concluded; her teachings had rendered the experience of penance (in the sense outlined in the previous section) impossible for those like himself. Instead, it led them to anxiety and to a preoccupation with dirty thoughts; to a state of "vain striving for assurance and comfort that they never find," which "must necessarily lead to despair and eternal damnation" (Luther, 1960c: 15.15). "Holy busywork," he called it. The penitent "runs to St. James, Rome, Jerusalem, here, there; prays to St. Brigit, this, that; fasts today, tomorrow, confesses here, there; asks this one, that one—and yet does not find peace" (Erikson, 1958: 219). "Some have ruined their bodies and gone out of their minds, thinking by virtue of their works to do away with their sins and soothe their heart" (Luther, 1960c: 10.4, 12.7).

Luther's revolt began in a criticism of traditional penance; it ended by rejecting the entire system of Roman Catholic jurisprudence: the confessional forum, moral casuistry, the priestly power to absolve guilt, Purgatory, the Treasury of Merits and the dispensary of indulgences, ecclesiastical courts, and inquisitions. After Luther, in the Protestant world at least, the church was depoliticized; political-economics, demoralized. This inaugurated a new stage in the history of the Western consciousness.

Notes

Preface

1. As a document of how "rational capital accounting" has been reconfigured by contemporary American sociologists into something other than bookkeeping, consider the following definition of the phrase by Randall Collins. Weber's concept, he writes, refers to "technology which is reduced to calculation to the largest possible degree" (Collins, 1980: 928), that is, "rationalized technology" (931). While this broadened characterization of the concept does not contradict Weber—DEB (double-entry bookkeeping) *is* a calculative technology—it does allow Collins tactically to avoid having to address the subject of bookkeeping itself. After all, machines are also rationalized technologies. In a later reconstruction of Weber's thesis, Collins in fact equates calculative technology with "mechanization" (Collins, 1986: 84, 86).

2. For an excellent critique of this proposition, see Thompson (1991).

3. As this book went to press, *Accounting, Auditing & Accountability Journal* (2004) published a special issue devoted to theological perspectives on accounting. It includes titles such as "Accounting, Love, and Justice," "Accounting and Theology" (which the authors describe as "initiating a dialogue between immediacy and eternity"), and "Sacred Vestiges in Financial Reporting: Mythical Readings Guided by Mircea Eliade."

Chapter One

1. A notable exception is Lutz Kaelber (1998). Jere Cohen agrees that modern capitalism had medieval precursors. However, he goes on to claim "that the religious factor played little or no part in the early rise of rational capitalism" (Cohen, 1980: 1352, 1351). The present book, obviously, challenges Cohen's position.

2. For a detailed, balanced analysis of Weber's sociology of medieval Catholicism, which Kaelber admits to having been "unevenly developed," see Kaelber (1998: 18–25, and Collins, 46–55). A readable, fair overview of Weber on Catholicism is also found in Collins (1986: 47– 89).

3. Sombart concedes Weber's point, but notes that Alberti represents an "old style," but nonetheless fully bourgeois life (Sombart, 1967: 154–59). Weber dismisses Alberti's influence by describing him as "a renaissance litterateur addressing himself to the humanistic aristocracy" (presumably unlike the yeoman Yankee, Benjamin Franklin) (Weber, 1958: 196, n. 12). Research shows on the contrary that Alberti's *Della Famiglia* was one of the most widely read and plagiarized works in Renaissance Italy (Ravenscroft, 1974).

Chapter Two

1. While agreeing with Watkins (1920) and McNeill (McNeill and Gamer, 1938) in other respects, Poschmann says, "it is wrong to exaggerate [the Celtic] connection and to regard monastic confession as the primary source of the entire later institution of penance"(Poschmann, 1964: 30). However, he concedes that confession was indeed understood by Church bishops to be radically different from the ancient canonical rite (131–32). Galtier (1937) explicitly denies that confessional penance originated in Ireland, but rather was derived directly from canonical penance. Poschmann vigorously disputes this (Poschmann, 1964: 133, n. 19; 133–34, n. 20; and 143, 145, 213). Tentler argues that while confession and canonical penance "openly clashed, they were fundamentally similar"(Tentler, 1977: 10). Nonetheless, he considers the enactment of compulsory confession in 1215 to have been a "momentous" event in Church history (22).

2. Examples of penitential literature in English: *Cursor Mundi* (Morris, 1961 [1847]), an encyclopedic poem composed ca. 1300–1325, part five of which contains a "Boke of Penance"; *The Book of Vices and Virtues* (Francis, 1968 [1942]), a translation of Lorens of Orleans, *Somme le Roi* (1279) (Lorens was confessor to King Philip the Fair. His summa was translated into six languages and published in eight English versions alone); the *Ancren Riwle* (Wilson, 1954), written ca. 1230 to three sisters who wished to be anchoresses;

Lay Folks' Catechism (Simmons and Nolloth, 1901); *Myrrour of Synneres and Speculum Peccatoris* (Page, 1976); and *The English Register of Godstow Nunnery* (Clark, 1905).

3. Unless otherwise specified, the following words and phrases are taken directly from *decreta* issued at the Fourth Lateran Council and at the Council of Trent (1551) (Denzinger, 1957: 173, secs. 437, 274–79, and 879–906).

Chapter Three

1. Delumeau claims that there is no "inevitable coincidence" between the "obsession neurosis" of moral scrupulosity and the sacrament of confession. Yet, he adds, it is "impossible . . . to deny" a connection between the two. "By making the confession of sin a fundamental . . . of the message of liberation, Christianity exposes the individual to morbid guilt" (Delumeau, 1990: 297).

2. This fact is the basis of Kaelber's (1998) attempt to emend Weber.

3. Weber claims that Catholic moral actuaries kept written accounts "as a sort of insurance premium" (Weber, 1958: 116). Elsewhere, he admits that Puritans did the same thing. Citing Baxter, he speaks about the Protestant practice of using "commercial similes" when describing eternal life. This, says Weber, "in effect makes man buy his own salvation"(Weber, 238, n. 102).

4. For more on Luther's scrupulosity and his critique of confession, see the appendix.

5. This should put to rest the still widely held belief (e.g., Tigar and Levy, 1977: 73–74) that the Arabic concept of place value was a precondition of DEB (double-entry bookkeeping).

Chapter Four

1. Pacioli's text was actually preceded thirty-six years by Bennedetto Cotrugli's treatment of DEB (double-entry bookkeeping) in his pamphlet on the art of commerce. However, this was not printed until late in the sixteenth century (Yamey, 1994; Raymond and Lopez, 1955: 375–77 and 414–16).

2. Given that for every debt created by the reception of a good or service, there is a corresponding credit, Roover asks, "is it then surprising that merchants would eventually hit upon a system founded on an equation between debits and credits?" (Florence de Roover, 1956: 115). Evidently there is, as indicated by the library of studies devoted to answering it.

3. That calculations of profit/loss, as done today, were of little interest in early modern bookkeeping texts is further indicated by the fact that both a firm's actual income and losses were distorted by the procedures recommended in them. First, there is no clear concept of inventory or equipment depreciation provided in the texts; instead, these maintain their original values over subsequent balances. Second, anticipated interest earnings on loans are credited to the company's cash account, even before they are received. Third, worthless accounts that will never be redeemed are put in a separate asset account known as doubtful accounts, and not posted as losses in the profit-loss account. This overstates the total assets and capital of the firm (Winjum, 1970: 748–49; Yamey, 1949: 108–9).

4. Probabilism is the name of the official medieval Church theory of casuistry. Its basic tenets are that only mathematics provides certain proofs; where certitude is not possible, as in morality, alternative opinions may be entertained; when choosing a course of action, one must prefer and act upon the "more probable," safer alternative (Nelson, 1981: 115–19).

5. Born into the *minuto popolo*, the "lower class," Pacioli's primary education took place in public religious schools overseen by Franciscan brothers. It was there that he was first introduced to grammar, rhetoric, and the art of notary (Taylor, 1942). Singularly ambitious, after graduating Pacioli began insinuating himself into the leading circles of the region around Florence, including the family of the prominent local merchant, Rompiasi (from whom he might well have first learned of DEB), and the Duke of Urbino. Urbino subsequently introduced Pacioli to Alberti, who for years thereafter served as Pacioli's personal tutor and companion. It was through Alberti that Pacioli would come into contact with the Church elite; and it was Alberti who encouraged Pacioli to take monastic vows, which Pacioli dutifully did, immediately upon his patron's death. Alberti's notions of business practice evidently influenced Pacioli as profoundly as those concerning the faith.

6. In his prosecution of Governor Verres (73–70 BCE) for theft of state funds, Cicero sarcastically admits that "we have heard of a man's never keeping accounts." But "it is far from satisfactory" (Cicero, 1953: II, i. 23.60). Later in the trial, he holds up Verres's sloppy records and rhetorically asks, "is this any way to present accounts?" "Confound the man's unscrupulous impudence" (14.36).

Chapter Five

1. The two standard works on this subject are McLaughlin (1939) and Noonan Jr. (1957). Nelson (1949), Weber (1958: 73–74 and 202–3, n. 29), and Tawney (1948: 28–54) offer sociological analyses of the subject. A more recent study is Le Goff (1979).

2. Pirenne relates the career of Godric of Finchale, Lincolnshire, a rapacious eleventh-century merchant adventurer who accumulated a great fortune only to entirely bequeath it to the Church in behalf of the poor, and become a hermit. For this he was canonized as a saint (Oakes, 1988–89: 85). For comparable examples of "merchant saints," see Vauchez (1994), Nelson (1949: 119), Florence de Roover (1957), and Raymond de Roover (1958: 18–19).

3. A profound sense of foreboding permeated late medieval life (Delumeau, 1990). This is reflected, among other ways, in the advice proffered in period home economics textbooks. Reasonably enough, all the texts enjoin prudence as a precondition of household management; but this is not the confident, hopeful, generous wisdom that might be expected of the men of faith who authored them. Instead, it is the grudging, worry-filled, gossipy cynicism of always expecting the worst. To cite just one example, at various places in *De Cura Rei Famuliari*, a pamphlet attributed to Bernard of Clairvuax (Lumby, 1965), the husband is warned against trusting idlers and jugglers, his household staff, close neighbors, distant strangers, those of a different social class than himself, and even his own sons and wife (whom "no medicine may mend him in this life"). As for women in general, "they are not so able to virtue as to sin which comes of them by kind and nature from their foremother Eve" (7.151–638). The recommended remedy for these and countless other human dangers is to "be awake all the time and be about" (7.167–68, 8.169–70): eternal vigilance.

An even more misanthropic tribute to the times is the book *On the Misery of the Human Condition* (1198). Extraordinarily popular—by 1650 it had been reprinted in all European languages and still survives today in 500 handwritten manuscripts (Lothario, 1969)—it was authored by Innocent III while he was still a cardinal. It allows us to understand why he was the perfect sponsor of legislation to mandate annual confession for all believers in 1215.

Chapter Six

1. In this ceremony, the receiving party struck a scale with an ingot of copper, symbolizing his acceptance of the thing, say a measure of olive oil, from the conveyor. This was said to "emancipate" the thing from its conveyor. If the commodity was a loan, then the creditor would conclude the agreement with the words, "you are condemned (*damnas* [to slavery]) to repay me money" (Weber, 1954: 108–9, n. 26; Jolowicz and Nicholas, 1972: 164–66).

2. There is extensive literature on medieval *artes dictandi*. Four of the best studies: Haskins (n.d.: 170–92), Kristeller (1979: 215–59), Kennedy (1980: 173–219), and Murphy (1974).

3. Weber, however, concludes that there was no Roman legal basis for the Florentine concept of general partnership (or what today is known as the joint stockholding company), the major capitalist enterprise during the medieval period. In spite of heroic efforts by Renaissance notaries to find such a precedent, "it did not fit the scheme of the Romanist view" (Weber, 2003: 175). Instead, the idea of general partnership, with a capital fund separate from the household that is therefore not liable for company debts, was a response "to concrete and existing circumstances" prevailing at the time (173).

Chapter Seven

1. Again: "In the name of God and the virgin Mary, may they give us to do things which turn to their praise and glory, to our honor and our profit for soul and body, Amen" (McGovern, 1970: 244, n. 115).

2. See Pacioli for other examples of "inner-worldly asceticism" (Pacioli, 1963: 34).

3. The standard French formulation reads, *Debiter celui et crediter celui qui donne* (Debit him who receives and credit him who

gives). Hugh Oldcastle in the first English bookkeeping text (1543) expresses the same idea this way: "All things receiued, or the receiuer must owe to all things deliuered, or to the deliuerer."

4. It is sometimes difficult for those untrained in bookkeeping to grasp how profit is possible if the total of credits always equals the total of debts. To say it simply, it is possible because profit is calculated by subtracting the total of the Revenue account from that of the Expense account. Since each sale and purchase is posted twice, as credit to one account and as a debit to another, then the books will balance even when there is a profit or loss. Usually, the revenues of a business are posted as a credit to Cash and simultaneously as a debit to Inventory. Expenses are booked as a debit to Cash and as a credit to Inventory.

The so-called Accounting Equation was developed well after Pacioli's death. It demonstrates even more clearly than the ledger the equitable nature of a business. Its simplest form: Assets = Equities. Assets are what the company in question has a legal claim on (what it owns); equities are the legal claims against the company (what it owes). Equities can either be held by outsiders to the company, such as creditors, in which case they are liabilities. Or, they can be held by company investors, in which case they are capital. Thus Assets = Liabilities + Capital; Capital = Assets − Liabilities.

5. Consider this advice from *The merchants Mirrour* (1636):

Q. "How booke you the Ready Money after the way of Debitor and Creditor?
A. "Cash [is] Debitor to Stock.
Q. "Why make you cash [a] Debitor?
A. "Because Cash (having received my money unto it) is obliged to restore it again at my pleasure: For Cash representeth (to me) a man, to whom I (only upon confidence) have put my money into his keeping, the which by reason is obliged to give back. . . ." (Littleton, 1933: 49–50)

6. Elsewhere Pacioli admits that "it does not [really] make any difference where the credit is posted" or what kinds of number system is used (Pacioli, 1963: 50 and 51).

Chapter Eight

1. There is an extensive literature concerning the supposed ideological support that the Church provided to early capitalism (see

Kaelber, 1998: 88–89, n. 64). However, it deals primarily with the moral teachings of lay preachers, notably the Franciscans. My argument is not addressed to the teachings as such (but see chapter 5), but to the ideological functions of a specific technology, namely, DEB.

2. See the appendix.

Appendix

1. This, in addition to "obsessive," "compulsive-obsessive," "morbidly obsessed," "confession[ally] compulsive," "compulsively retentive," "compensa[torily] compulsive," "compulsive[ly] addictive," "monastic[ally] compulsive," and "spiritually constipated" (an allegation Erikson suppports by pointing to Luther's actual constipation). Says Erikson, Luther suffered from "anxiety neurosis," "borderline psychosis," "ritualization," "asceticism," and plain old "monkery." He adds that Luther had a "suspicious severity," experienced "fanatic inner struggles," "neurotic exaggerations," "confessional scruples," and "hyperconscientiousness."

2. The Church defended herself against Luther's accusation that penance is a "torture of conscience" (Denzinger, 1957: 276, sec. 900).

References

Alberti, Leon Battista. 1971. *Della Famiglia*, translated and edited by Guido Guarino. Cranbury, New Jersey: Associated University Presses.

Alighieri, Dante. 1958. *The Divine Comedy*, translated by Lawrence White. New York: Pantheon Books.

Alphonsus of Liguori, Saint. 1905. *Moral Theology*, translated by P. Guadi. Rome.

Aristotle. 1954. *Rhetoric*, translated by Rhys Roberts. New York: Modern Library.

Arrington, C. Edward and J. Francis. 1993. "Giving Economic Accounts: Accounting as a Cultural Practice." *Accounting Organizations and Society* 18: 107–24.

Augustine, Saint. 1972. *Concerning the City of God against the Pagans*, translated by Henry Bettenson, introduced by David Knowles. New York: Penguin Books.

Barkan, Leonard. 1975. *Nature's Work of Art*. New Haven, Connecticut: Yale University Press.

Baron, Hans. 1938. "Franciscan Poverty and Civic Wealth as Factors in the Rise of Hunanistic Thought." *Speculum* 13: 1–37.

Baxandall, Michael. 1971. *Giotto and the Orators*. London: Oxford University Press.

Becker, Ernest. 1975. *Escape from Evil*. New York: Free Press.

Berman, Harold. 1983. *Law and Revolution: The Formation of the Western Legal Tradition*. Cambridge: Harvard University Press.

Bernard, Abbot of Clairvaux. 1964. *The Steps of Humility*, translated by Robert Gleason. Garden City, New York: Image Books.

Bertman, Stephen. 1999. *Hyperculture: The Human Cost of Speed*. Westport, Connecticut: Praeger.

Bloomfield, Morton. 1955. "A Preliminary List of Incipits of Latin Works on the Virtues and Vices, Mainly of the Thirteenth, Fourteenth and Fifteenth Centuries." *Traditio* 11: 260–379.

———. 1952. *The Seven Deadly Sins*. East Lansing: Michigan State University Press.

Boyle, Leonard. 1974. "The Summa Confessorum of John of Freiburg and the Popularization of the Moral Teaching of St. Thomas and of Some of His Contemporaries." *St. Thomas Aquinas Commemorative Studies*. Toronto.

Bryan, William F. and Germaine Dempster, eds. 1958. *Sources and Analogues of Chaucer's Canterbury Tales*. New York: Humanities Press.

Bryer, R. A. 1993. "Double-Entry Bookkeeping and the Birth of Capitalism." *Critical Perspectives on Accounting* 4: 113–40.

Burckhardt, Jacob. 1928. *The Civilisation of the Renaissance in Italy*, translated by S. G. C. Middlemore. New York: Macmillan.

Butler-Dowdon, ed. 1944. *The Book of Margery Kempe*. New York: Devin-Adair Co.

Carruthers, Bruce and Wendy Espeland. 1991. "Accounting for Rationality: Double-Entry Bookkeeping and the Rhetoric of Economic Rationality." *American Journal of Sociology* 97: 31–69.

Chatfield, Michael. 1974. *A History of Accounting Thought*. Hinsdale, Illinois: Dryden Press.

Cheney, C. R. 1931. "The Papal Legate and English Monasteries in 1206." *English Historical Review* 46: 443–52.

Ciarrocchi, Joseph 1995. *The Doubting Disease: Help for Scrupulosity and Religious Compulsions*. Mahwah, New Jersey: Paulist Press.

Cicero, Marcus Tullius. 1949. *De Inventione*, translated by H. M. Hubbell. Cambridge: Harvard University Press.

———. 1942. *De Partitione Oratoria*, translated by H. Rackham. Cambridge: Harvard University Press.

———. 1953. *The Verrine Orations*, translated by L. H. G. Greenwood. Cambridge: Harvard University Press.

Clark, Andrew, ed. 1905. *The English Register of Godstow Nunnery.* London: Kegan Paul, Trench, Tubner & Co.

Cohen, Jere. 1980. "Rational Capitalism in Renaissance Italy." *American Journal of Sociology* 85: 1340–55.

Colignon, Richard and Mark Covaleski. 1991. "A Weberian Framework for the Study of Accounting." *Accounting, Organizations and Society* 16: 141–57.

Colinson, Robert. 1638. *Idea Rationaria or the Perfect Accomptant.* Edinburgh, Scotland: David Lindsey.

Collins, Randall. 1986. *Max Weber: A Skeleton Key.* London and Beverly Hills: Sage.

———. 1980. "Weber's Last Theory of Capitalism: A Systematization." *American Sociological Review* 45: 925–45.

Columban. 1938. "The Penitential of Columban." In *Medieval Handbooks of Penance,* translated by John McNeill and Helena Gamer. New York: Columbia University Press.

Delumeau, Jean. 1990. *Sin and Fear: The Emergence of a Western Guilt Culture,* translated by Eric Nicholson. New York: Macmillan.

Denzinger, Heinrich. 1957. *The Sources of Catholic Dogma,* translated by Roy Deferrari. St. Louis, Missouri: Herder.

Dondain, A. 1937. "La Somme de Simon de Hinton." *Reserchers de Theologies Ancienne et Medieval* 9: no pages.

East, James. 1968. "Brunetto Latini's Rhetoric of Letter Writing." *Quarterly Journal of Speech* 54: 240–46.

Ehrenberg, Richard. 1928. *Capital and Finance during the Age of the Renaissance,* translated by H. M. Lucas. London: Jonathan Cape.

Erikson, Erik. 1958. *Young Man Luther: A Study in Psychoanalysis and History.* New York: Norton.

Faulhaber, Charles. 1974. "*The Summa Dictaminis* of Guido Faba." In *Rhetoric of the Middle Ages,* edited by James Murphy. Berkeley: University of California Press.

Finnian. 1938. "The Penitential of Finnian." In *Medieval Handbooks of Penance*, translated by John McNeill and Helena Gamer. New York: Columbia University Press.

Foucault, Michel. 1978. *The History of Sexuality*, vol. 1, translated by Robert Hurley. New York: Pantheon.

———. 1988. "Technologies of the Soul." In *Technologies of the Soul*, edited by Luther Martin, Huck Gutman, and Patrick Hutton. Amherst: University of Massachusetts.

Francis, W. Nelson, trans. 1968 (1942). *The Book of Vices and Virtues*. London: Percey Lund, Humphries & Co.

Friedman, Milton. 1970. "The Social Responsibility of Business Is to Increase its Profits." *New York Times Magazine*, Sept. 13.

Gallhofer, S. and J. Haslam. 1991. "The Aura of Accounting in the Context of a Crisis: Germany and the First World War." *Accounting, Organizations and Society* 16: 487–520.

Galtier. 1937. "De la Penitence Latine à la Penitence Celtique." *Revue d'Histoire Ecclesiasa* (no vol.): 277–306.

Geijsbeek, John. 1914. *Ancient Double-Entry Bookkeeping*. Houston: Scholar's Book Co.

Gleick, James. 1999. *Faster: The Acceleration of Just about Everything*. New York: Pantheon.

Gower, John. 1963. *Confessio Amantis*, translated by Terence Tiller. Baltimore, Maryland: Penguin Books.

Haering, Bernard. 1963. "The Phenomenology of the Scrupulous Conscience." In *The Law of Christ*, translated by Edwin Haiser. Cork, Ireland: Mercier Press.

Haskins, Charles. n.d. "The Early *Artes dictandi* in Italy." In *Studies in Medieval Culture*. New York: Ungar.

Have, O. ten. 1956. "Simon Stevin of Bruges." In *Studies in the History of Accounting*, edited by A. C. Littleton and B. S. Yamey. Homewood, Illinois: Richard Irwin.

Hines, Ruth. 1988. "Financial Accounting: In Communicating Reality, We Construct Reality." *Accounting, Organizations and Society* 13: 251–61.

Hopwood, Anthony. 1983. "On Trying to Study Accounting in the Contexts in which It Operates." *Accounting, Organizations and Society* 8: 287–305.

Hugo of Saint Victor. 1961. *Didascalicon*, translated by Jerome Taylor. New York: Columbia University Press.

Ignatius of Loyola, Saint. 1964. "Notes Concerning Scruples." In the *Spiritual Exercises of St. Ignatius*, translated by Anthony Mottola. Garden City, New York: Doubleday.

Jackson, J. G. C. 1956. "The History of Methods of Exposition of Double-entry Book-Keeping in England." In *Studies in the History of Accounting*, edited by A. C. Littleton and B. S. Yamey. Homewood, Illinois: Richard Irwin.

Jacobs, Kerry and S. Walker. 2000. "Accounting and Accountability in the Iona Community." Proceedings of the Sixth International Interdisciplinary Perspectives on Accounting Conference, Manchester, England.

Jolowicz, Herbert and Barry Nicholas. 1972. *Historical Introduction to the Study of Roman Law*. London: Cambridge University Press.

Jones, P. J. 1956. "Florentine Families and Florentine Dairies in the Fourteenth Century." *British School at Rome* 24: 183–205.

Kaelber, Lutz. 1998. *Schools of Asceticism*. University Park: Pennsylvania State University Press.

Kats, P. 1930. "A Surmise Regarding the Origin of Bookkeeping by Double-entry." *Accounting Review* 5: 311–16.

Kennedy, George. 1980. *Classical Rhetoric and its Christian and Secular Tradition from Ancient to Modern Times*. Durham: University of North Carolina Press.

Kent, Francis. 1977. *Household and Lineage in Renaissance Florence*. Princeton: Princeton University Press.

Kristeller, Paul. 1979. *Renaissance Thought and its Sources*. New York: Columbia University Press.

Kuczynaski, Jurgen. 1968. "Sombart, Werner." In *Encyclopedia of the Social Sciences*. New York: Macmillan.

Kuhn, Thomas. 1970. *The Structure of Scientific Revolutions.* Chicago: University of Chicago Press.

Lamond, Elizabeth, trans. 1890. *Walter of Henley's Husbandry Together with an Anonymous Husbandry, Seneschaucie and Robert Grosseteste's Rules.* London: Longmans, Green & Co.

Landucci, Lucca. 1927. *A Florentine Diary from 1450–1516*, translated by Alice de Rosen Jervis. New York: Dutton.

Lasko, Ernest. 1949. "A Psychotherapy for Scruples." *Homiletic and Pastoral Review* 49: 617–23, 906–14.

Latini, Brunetto. 1948. *Li Livres Dou Tresor*, translated and edited by Francis Carmody. Berkeley: University of California Press.

Leff, Michael. 1978. "Boethius' *De Differentiis Topicis*, Book IV." In *Medieval Eloquence*, edited by James Murphy. Berkeley: University of California Press.

Le Goff, Jacques. 1979. "The Usurer and Purgatory." In *The Dawn of Modern Banking*, Center for Medieval and Renaissance Studies, Los Angeles. New Haven, Connecticut: Yale University Press .

Littleton, A. C. 1933. *Accounting Evolution to 1900.* New York: American Institute Publishing Co.

Littleton, A. C. and V. K. Zimmerman. 1962. *Accounting Theory: Continuity and Change.* Englewood Cliffs, New Jersey: Prentice-Hall.

Lopez, Robert. 1979. "Introduction." In *The Dawn of Modern Banking*, Center for Medieval and Renaissance Studies, Los Angeles. New Haven, Connecticut: Yale University Press.

Lord, Daniel and Francis O'Boyle. 1932. *Are You Scrupulous?* St. Louis, Missouri: Queen's Work Press.

Lotario dei Segni. 1969. *On the Misery of the Human Condition*, translated by Margaret Mary Dietz, edited by Donald Howard. New York: Bobbs.

Lumby, J. Rawson, ed. 1965. *Bernardus de cura rei famuliaris.* London: Oxford University Press.

Luther, Martin. 1960a. "The Babylonian Captivity of the Church." In *Luther's Works*, vol. 36, edited by Helmut T. Lehmann. Philadelphia: Muhlenberg Press.

———. 1960b. "To John von Staupitz Wittenberg, May 30, 1515." In *Luther's Works*, vol. 48, edited by Helmut T. Lehmann. Philadelphia: Muhlenberg Press.

———. 1960c. "The Sacrament of Penance, 1519." In *Luther's Works*, vol. 35, edited by Helmut T. Lehmann. Philadelphia: Muhlenberg Press.

MacKinnon, H. 1969. "William de Montibus, A Medieval Teacher." In *Essays in Medieval History Presented to Bertie Wilkinson*, edited by T. A.Sandquist and M. R. Powicke. Toronto.

McMahan, John W. 1939. "Relation of the Concept of Accounting Cost to Accounting Knowledge." Ph.D. dissertation, Champaign: University of Illinois.

Maltby, Josephine. 1997. "Accounting and the Soul of the Middle Class; Gustav Freytag's *Soll Und Haben*." *Accounting, Organizations and Society* 22: 69–87.

Martin, Alfred von. 1936. *Sociology of the Renaissance*, translated by Wallace Ferguson. New York: Harper.

Martin, Luther, Huck Gutman, and Patrick Hutton, eds. 1988. *Technologies of Self: A Seminar with Michel Foucault*. Amherst: University of Massachusetts Press.

Martines, Julia, trans. 1967. *Two Memoirs of Renaissance Florence: The Diaries of Buonaccorso Pitti and Gregoria Dati*. New York: Harper.

Mauss, Marcel. 1954. *Gift Functions of Exchange in Archaic Societies*. Glencoe, Illinois: Free Press.

McClosky, D. 1986. *The Rhetoric of Economics*. Brighton, England: Wheatsheaf.

McGovern, John. 1970. "The Rise of New Economic Attitudes . . . During the Later Middle Ages and the Renaissance." *Traditio* 26: 217–53.

McLaughlin, T. P. 1939. "The Teaching of the Canonists on Usury." *Medieval Studies* 1: 87–141.

McNeill, John. 1932a. *The Celtic Penitentials and Their Influence on Continental Christianity*. Paris.

——. 1934. "Historical Types of Method in the Cure of Souls." *Crozier Quarterly* 10: 323–24.

——. 1932b. "Medicine for Sin as Prescribed in the Penitentials. *Church History* 1: 14–26.

McNeill, John and Helena Gamer, trans. 1938. *Medieval Handbooks of Penance*. New York: Columbia University Press.

Melis, Federigo. 1950. *Storia della Ragioneria*. Bolgna, Italy.

Michaud-Quantin, Pierre. 1962. *Sommes de Casuistique et Manuels de Confession au Moyen Age*. Montreal: Librarie Dominicaine.

Miller, J. M., trans. 1973. "The Flowers of Rhetoric." In *Readings in Medieval Rhetoric*, edited by J. M. Miller, Michael Prosser, and Thomas Benson. Bloomington: Indiana University Press.

Miller, Peter and Christopher Napier. 1993. "Genealogies of Calculation." *Accounting, Organizations and Society* 18: 631–47.

Miller, Peter and O'Leary, Ted. 1987. "Accounting and the Construction of the Governable Person." *Accounting, Organizations and Society* 12: 235–65.

Mills, Gregory. 1994. "Early Accounting in Northern Italy." *Accounting Historians Journal* 21: 81–96.

Mitchell, Gerard. 1955. "The Origins of Irish Penance." *Irish Theological Quarterly* 22.

Mitchell, A., P. Sikka, and H. Willmott. 1998. "Sweeping it under the Carpet: The Role of Accounting Firms in Money-Laundering." *Accounting, Organizations and Society* 23: 689–607.

Morgan, Glenn and H. Willmott, H. 1993. "The 'New' Accounting Research." *Accounting, Auditing & Accountability Journal* 6: 3–36.

Morris, Richard, ed. 1961 (1847). *Cursor Mundi*. London: Oxford University Press.

Most, Kenneth. 1976. "How Wrong Was Sombart?" *Accounting Historians Journal* 3: 22–28.

——. 1972. "Sombart's Propositions Revisited." *Accounting Review* 47: 722–34.

Murphy, James. 1967. "Cicero's Rhetoric in the Middle Ages." *Quarterly Journal of Speech* 53: 334–41.

———. 1974. *Rhetoric in the Middle Ages.* Berkeley: University of California Press.

Nelson, Benjamin. 1981. *On the Roads to Modernity,* edited by Toby Huff. Totowa, New Jersey: Rowman & Littlefield.

———. 1949. *The Idea of Usury.* Princeton, New Jersey: Princeton University Press.

———. 1947. "The Usurer and the Merchant Prince," *Journal of Economic History,* supp. 7: 104–22.

Noonan Jr., John. 1957. *The Scholastic Analysis of Usury.* Cambridge: Harvard University Press.

Nussbaum, Frederick. 1937. *A History of the Economic Institutions of Modern Europe.* New York: F. S. Crofts.

Oakes, Guy. 1988–89. "Farewell to the Protestant Ethic?" *Telos* 78: 81–94.

Oschinsky, Dorothea. 1956. "Medieval Treatises on Estate Accounting." In *Studies in The History of Accounting,* edited by A. C. Littleton and B. S. Yamey. Homewood, Ilinois: Richard Irwin.

———. 1971. *Walter of Henley and other Treatises on Estate Management and Accounting.* London: Oxford University Press.

Oppenheim, A. Leo. 1964. *Ancient Mesopotamia.* Chicago: University of Chicago Press.

Origo, Iris. 1957. *The Merchant of Prato: Francesco di Marco Datini 1335–1410.* New York: Knopf.

Orsy, Ladislas. 1978. *The Evolving Church and the Sacrament of Penance.* Denville, New Jersey: Dimension Books.

Pacioli, Luca. 1963. *Paciolo on Accounting,* translated and introduced by Gene Brown and Kenneth Johnston. New York: McGraw-Hill.

Paden, William. 1988. "Theaters of Humility and Suspicion." In *Technologies of the Self,* edited by Luther Martin, Huck Gutman, and Patrick Hutton. Amherst: University of Massachusetts Press.

Page, Cornelius, trans. 1976. *The Myrrour of Synneres and Speculum Peccatoris*. Dobbs Ferry, New York: Mercy College.

Patterson, Lee. 1978. "The 'Parson's Tale' and the Quitting of the Canterbury Tales." *Traditio* 34: 331–80.

Pellicani, Luciano. 1989. "Reply to Guy Oakes." *Telos* 81: 63–76.

Peragallo, Edward. 1956. "Origin of the Trial Balance." In *Studies in the History of Accounting*, edited by A. C. Littleton and B. S. Yamey. Homewood, Illinois: Richard Irwin.

Petrarch, Francesco. 1967. *Four Dialogues for Scholars*, translated and edited by Conrad Rawski. Cleveland: Western Reserve University Press.

Pieper, Josef. 1966. *The Four Cardinal Virtues*, translated by Daniel Coogan, Lawrence Lynch, Richard Winston, and Clara Winston. Notre Dame, Indiana: Notre Dame University Press.

Pirenne, Henri. 1937. *Economic and Social History of Medieval Europe*. New York: Harcourt, Brace and World.

Poschmann, Bernard. 1964. *Penances and the Anointing of the Sick*, translated by Francis Courtney. New York: Herder and Herder.

Power, M. and Laughlin, R. 1992. "Critical Theory and Accounting." In *Critical Management Studies*, edited by M. Alvesson and H. Hillmott. London: Sage.

Power, Eileen, trans. 1928. *The Goodman of Paris*. London: Routledge & Sons.

Pseudo-Cicero. 1918. *Rhetorica ad Herennium*, translated by Harry Caplan. Cambridge: Harvard University Press.

Rand, Ayn. 1961. *The Virtue of Selfishness: A New Concept of Egoism*. New York: Times-Mirror.

Rashdall, Hastings. 1936. *The Universities of Europe in the Middle Ages*, vol. 1, edited by F. M. Powicke and A. B. Emden. London: Oxford University Press.

Ravenscroft, J. 1974. "The Third Book of Alberti's *Della Famiglia* and its Two *Rifacimenti*." *Italian Studies* 24: 45–53.

Raymond, Irving and Robert Lopez. 1955. *Medieval Trade in the Mediterranean World*. New York: Columbia University Press.

Reik, Theodor. 1959. *The Compulsion to Confess*, translated by Katherine Jones. New York: Farrar, Straus & Cuddahy.

Robertson, D. and Huppe Bernard, eds. 1951. *Piers Plowman and Scriptural Tradition*. Princeton, New Jersey: Princeton University Press.

Robertson Jr., D. W. 1946. "A Note on the Classical Origin of "Circumstances' in the Medieval Confessional." *Studies in Philology* 42: 6–14.

Roover, Florence de. 1956. "Partnership Accounts in Twelfth Century Genoa." In *Studies in the History of Accounting*, edited by A. C. Littleton and B. S. Yamey. Homewood, Illinois: Richard Irwin.

———. 1957. "Restitution in Renaissance Florence." In *Studi in Onore de Armando Sapori*. Milan.

Roover, Raymond de. 1944. "Early Accounting Problems of Foreign Exchange." *Accounting Review* 19: 381–406.

———. 1943. "The Lingering Influence of Medieval Practices." *Accounting Review* 18: 148–51.

———. 1955. "New Perspectives on the History of Accounting." *Accounting Review* 30: 405–20.

———. 1963. *The Rise and Decline of the Medici Bank*. Cambridge: Harvard University Press.

———. 1958. "The Story of the Alberti Company of Florence, 1302–1348 as Revealed in Its Account Books." *Business History Review* 32: 14–59.

Santa, Thomas M. 1999. *Understanding Scrupulosity*. Liguori, Missouri: Liguori Pub.

Sapori, Armando. 1953. "The Culture of the Medieval Italian Merchant." In *Enterprise and Secular Change*, edited by Frederic Lane. Homewood, Illinois: Richard Irwin.

Scheel, Otto. 1929. *Dokumente zu Luthers Entwicklung*. Tübingen, Germany: J. C. B. Mohr.

Scribner, Robert. 1993. "The Reformation, Popular Magic, and the 'Disenchantment of the World.'" *Journal of Interdisciplinary History* 23: 475–94.

Simmons and Nolloth, eds. 1901. *Lay Folks' Catechism*. London: Oxford University Press.

Smith, Charles. 1951. *Innocent III: Church Defender*. Baton Rouge: Louisiana State University Press.

Smith C. A. 1954, "Speculations on Roman Influence on the Theory of Double-entry Bookkeeping." *Accounting Research* 5: 335–42.

Snape, R. H. 1926. *English Monastic Finances in the Later Middle Ages*. London: Cambridge University Press.

Sombart, Werner. 1924. *Der Moderne Kapitalismus*, sixth ed. Munich and Leipzig.

———. 1967. *The Quintessence of Capitalism*, translated by M. Epstein. New York: Howard Fertig.

Ste. Croix, Geoffrey de. 1956. "Greek and Roman Accounting." In *Studies in the History Of Accounting*, edited by A. C. Littleton and B. S. Yamey. Homewood, Illinois: Richard Irwin.

Stern, Randolph. 1971. "Francesco Guicciardini and His Brothers." In *Renaissance Studies in Honor of Hans Baron*, edited by A. Molho and J. A. Tedeschi. Dekalb: Northern Illinois University Press.

Stone, E. 1962. "Profit-and-Loss Accountancy at Norwich Cathedral Priory." *Royal Historical Society Transactions* 12: 34–38.

Tawney, Richard. 1948. *Religion and the Rise of Capitalism*. London: John Murray.

Taylor, Emmett. 1956. "Luca Pacioli." In *Studies in the History of Accounting*, edited by A. C. Littleton and B. S. Yamey. Homewood, Illinois: Richard Irwin.

———. 1942. *No Royal Road: Luca Pacioli and His Times*. Chapel Hill: North Carolina University Press.

Tentler, Thomas. 1977. *Sin and Confession on the Eve of the Reformation*. Princeton: Princeton University Press.

Thompson, Grahame. 1991. "Is Accounting Rhetorical? Methodology, Luca Pacioli and Printing." *Accounting, Organizations and Society* 16: 572–99.

Thompson, S. Harrison. 1940. *The Writings of Robert Grosseteste.* London: Cambridge University Press.

Tigar, Michael and Levy. 1977. *Law and the Rise of Capitalism.* New York: Monthly Review Press.

Troeltsch, Ernst. 1960. *The Social Teachings of the Christian Churches*, vol. 1, translated by Olive Wyon. New York: Harper.

Usher, Payson. 1943. *The Early History of Deposit Banking in Mediterranean Europe.* London: Cambridge University Press.

Vauchez, Andre. 1994. *The Laity in the Middle Ages*, translated by Margery Schneider. Notre Dame, Indiana: Notre Dame University Press.

Walker, S. P. 1998. "How to Secure Your Husband's Esteem. Accounting and Private Patriarchy . . ." *Accounting, Organizations and Society* 23: 485–514.

Watkins, O. D. 1920. *A History of Penance*, 2 vols. London: Longman, Green & Co.

Weber, Marianne. 1975. *Max Weber: A Biography*, translated by H. Zorn. New York: Wiley.

Weber, Max. 1946. "Bureaucracy." In *From Max Weber*, translated and edited by Hans Gerth and C. Wright Mills. New York: Oxford University Press.

———. 1950. *General Economic History*, translated by Frank Knight. Glencoe, Illinois: Free Press.

———. 2003. *The History of Commercial Partnerships in the Middle Ages*, translated and introduced by Lutz Kaelber. New York: Rowman & Littlefield.

———. 1954. *On Law in Economy and Society*, translated by Edward Shils and Max Rheinstein. New York: Simon & Schuster.

———. 1958. *The Protestant Ethic and the Spirit of Capitalism*, translated by Talcott Parsons. New York: Scribner.

———. 1963. *The Sociology of Religion*, translated by Ephraim Fischoff. Boston: Beacon.

———. 1947. *The Theory of Social and Economic Organizations*, translated and edited by A. M. Henderson and Talcott Parsons. New York: Free Press.

Wenzel, S. 1976. "Vices, Virtues, and Popular Preaching," no. 6 in *Medieval and Renaissance Studies*, edited by Dale Randall. Durham, North Carolina: Duke University Press.

Wilson, R. M., ed. 1954. *The Ancren Riwle*. London: Oxford University Press.

Winjum, James. 1970. "Accounting in Its Age of Stagnation." *Accounting Review* 45: 743–61.

Yamey, Basil. 1964. "Accounting and the Rise of Capitalism: Further Notes on a Theme by Sombart." *Journal of Accounting Research* 2: 117–36.

———. 1994. "Benedetto Cotrugli." *Accounting, Business & Financial History* 4: 43–50.

———. 1967. "Fifteenth and Sixteenth Century Manuscripts on the Art of Bookkeeping." *Journal of Accounting Research* 5: 51–76.

———. 1930. "The Functional Development of Double-Entry Bookkeeping." *Accountant* 103: 333–42.

———. 1974. "Pious Inscriptions; Confused Accounts; Classifications of Accounts: Three Historical Notes." In *Debits, Credits, Finance and Profits*, edited by B. S. Yamey and H. Edey. London: Sweet and Maxwell.

———. 1949. "Scientific Bookkeeping and the Rise of Capitalism." *Economic History Review*, second series 1: 99–113.

Yamey, B. S. and Parker, R. H, eds. 1994. *Accounting History: Some British Contributions*. New York: Oxford University Press.

Zimmerman, T. C. Price. 1971. "Confession and Autobiography." In *Renaissance Studies in Honor of Hans Baron*, edited by A. Molho and J. A Tedeschi. Dekalb: Northern Illinois University Press.

Index